D0258008

Never Afraid to Miss

Never Afraid to Miss

MALCOLM MACDONALD
with
BRIAN WOOLNOUGH

CASSELL
LONDON

Also by Malcolm Macdonald

Win! (Pelham Books)
Football Makes Me Laugh (Pelham Books)

CASSELL LTD.
35 Red Lion Square, London WC1R 4SG
and at Sydney, Auckland, Toronto, Johannesburg,
an affiliate of
Macmillan Publishing Co., Inc.,
New York.

Copyright © Malcolm Macdonald 1980
Cartoons © Clive Collins 1980

All rights reserved. No part of this publication
may be reproduced, stored in a retrieval system,
or transmitted, in any form or by any means,
electronic, mechanical, photocopying, recording or
otherwise, without the prior permission of
Cassell Ltd.

First published 1980

ISBN 0 304 30639 8

Printed in Great Britain by
Hazell, Watson & Viney Ltd.
Aylesbury, Bucks

CONTENTS

ILLUSTRATIONS

Introduction

This is not an autobiography. How could it be? When my good friend Brian Woolnough and I first sat down to discuss it I was 30 years old. The definition of autobiography in the English Dictionary is: The life of a person written by himself. My life has only just begun, there is so much more I want to achieve, discover and do — inside and out of football. No, this book is all about my ten years in soccer as a player. It is controversial, will upset people, please many and intrigue others. It is, of course, the truth. But how could I call it the story of my life when there is so much about the running of our great game I don't understand and so many questions I would like answered? I have always thought that the people worst treated in football are the men that matter, the players. Without players there would be no sport and yet we are just pawns in a very big, powerful business. I was just another player with his head in the clouds until I wanted to leave Newcastle. I wrote to them twice, challenging the club legally over their right to hold me to a year's option on my already completed contract. I was ready to take Newcastle to court and quit the game if I had lost the case. It was then I received three anonymous phone calls warning me to drop any action I had planned. Fortunately I didn't have to go ahead, as Newcastle didn't reply to my letters and I was sold to Arsenal. But those heavy phone calls only sent me off on a trail for the truth. Why shouldn't a player be able to fight for what he deserves, why is he treated like a puppet with big brother pulling the strings? I am still searching for many of the answers and the men in power don't encourage people like me to pry around. Are they afraid of what I might find? I'm certain that half of the registered players in this country don't understand their contracts or know their rights. Believe me, they don't have many, and I detail my fears and hopes in Chapter 18. I have also big ambitions in business and plans for my family. My four daughters are so young I couldn't tell you what the future holds for them. So that is why I refuse to call this book an autobiography, simply because it is the complete story of only one part of my life.

1

Finished at twenty-nine

The pain was sudden and excruciating. There had been no real warning and yet as I lay face down, my left knee bent underneath me like a piece of twisted rubber, I knew I was finished.

I had always wanted to end my career at Wembley, St James' Park or Highbury, in front of the people who had acclaimed my goals and turned my dreams into reality. There were no familiar faces in the grey Elfsborg Stadium in Sweden, only a few thousand people watching their local team take on Djurgaarden, a club I joined on loan for the summer of 1979.

With five minutes to go I had been put through with only the goalkeeper to beat. It was a classic situation for me; clear of the defence, the goal at my mercy and the ball on my favourite left foot. I had already scored in the game and this would be the winner. I was confident, I couldn't miss. Suddenly I collapsed in agony and watched in horror as the ball rolled gently towards the surprised goalkeeper. I can still see his eyes, opening in amazement at his good fortune. It is funny how much can pass through your mind in a split second; a million things seemed to spin around. The sudden fear of never playing again, memories, people, goals all flashed across the screen in front of my eyes. Jackie Milburn had once said to me: 'Because you're a striker, always leave a little bit of fitness in store for the last seconds of the game'. At that moment I had nothing left. My knee, my damned left knee again, was locked and my body was drained.

On the train journey home across Sweden I sat alone, sipping a beer, thinking, half listening to the jokes and friendly conversation. It was a long and lonely trip. I thought to myself: 'Imagine doing that at Old Trafford in front of 55,000 fans, I would be a laughing stock'. I began to plan my future and the longer the train rattled into the night the more I realized that Malcolm Macdonald was finished at 29. I would go home and tell Arsenal manager Terry Neill that I knew I would never be the same again.

The stupid thing is, I had gone to Sweden to get completely fit. A few months earlier in January I had undergone my fourth cartilage operation, the second on my left knee in five months. I thought my troubles were behind me and my nightmare was over. Arsenal don't like loan transfers for their players but Terry Neill and the board admitted that Sweden would be good for me. I could get match fit, regain my confidence and go back to Highbury ready to open a new chapter of goalscoring. I had played some reserve matches in the second half of the 1978-79 season, been in the FA Cup Final squad and even scored against Chelsea in the last game at Stamford Bridge on the Monday following our victory over Manchester United. Sweden however was a big disappointment. I didn't improve enough, my knee wouldn't withstand the pressure and I began to make excuses for my form ....

Then, after the disastrous incident in Elfsborg, the club surgeon Christian Akarmark hit me between the eyes with these words of advice: 'I have been watching you closely in matches. In my opinion you are killing yourself. Go home, you are not doing yourself any good.'

All the way back to London I tossed over in my mind what to tell Terry Neill. It is very hard for a player to admit to his manager that he is injured, let alone finished. I decided to say I couldn't possibly last a full season, I could maybe give the club 25 matches, perhaps in a different position. For some reason Neill didn't believe me, he wouldn't accept that I was heading for the scrapheap.

We met at London Colney where he was discussing the build-up to the new season with trainer Fred Street. Terry just said: 'Let's see how it goes'. I looked at Street for support, pleading with him to back me up. I knew. How could they judge what my knee was like? All that happened was I had to do three days' training in preparation for a pre-season tour of Germany. Three days! That was a joke. I knew the first real test would be too much for my left knee. We were to cover as much ground on a zig-zag course as possible in twelve minutes. I was hobbling from the start, dragging my leg behind me. It was embarrassing for me and the other players. I thought someone would stop me. Neill and his entire coaching staff just looked on; I felt like screaming at them: 'For God's sake' what more do I have to do?

Do you want me in this club? What is going to happen?'

Arsenal still wasted the fare on sending me to Germany. I had no chance of training properly or playing. On the first day we gathered beneath a huge, steep side of a mountain nicknamed 'Cardiac Hill'. We had to sprint up one side and race down the other. At the top I was in so much pain I felt like crying. Going down I was physically sick. I was the last to finish and just crawled back to the clubhouse. 'Someone please send me home', I said, 'I am not going on like this.'

Back in London, I had to wait five days to see Nigel Harris, the club's knee specialist who had operated on me three times. There was no need for him to examine me. I just said: 'I am not going to make a fool of myself any more'. He nodded and in a couple of minutes a decision had been made that deep down I knew in Sweden. The medical diagnosis of my injury is osteo-arthritis of the left knee. It means that pieces of bone flake off and damage the joints.

The air seemed clearer when I left Harris. I went for a walk, not planning my route, just strolling blindly around. I needed to be alone. Suddenly I could plan the future. I remember the day clearly. It was Thursday, 2 August, the first day of the Lord's Test Match. On Friday I went to watch the cricket with some friends and it rained all day. Usually when it rains at a cricket ground you drink. That day was no exception and we ended up at a local rugby club. I got drunk, not for the first time in my life, but somehow it was significant. Alex Montgomery, a sports writer with *The Sun* newspaper, came to see me and asked me if my career was finished. There was so much I wanted to say but I was too drunk to explain. I just said something like, 'The party is over'. On reflection there was not much more to add.

The next morning reality struck. I was finished. Ten years of goals, ten years of glory were over. I just lay in bed asking myself questions. Would I miss it? There would be no more excitement of match days, no chance to go back to Wembley. I would miss my daily train journey from Bedford to St Pancras with break-fast of coffee and toast and a game of crib with the same lads. But I have always been a realist. I never believe good things go on forever. I packed a lot into my career: happiness, pain, mystery, controversy, friends, enemies. There would surely be more chapters ahead. I had always wanted to do more with my life than just play football.

The one lesson my career has taught me is never delay a

cartilage operation and always give yourself enough time to recover. The ideal time is ten to twelve weeks. Kevin Beattie, Ipswich Town's brilliant England international defender, returned after only about a month and paid the penalty. His knee wasn't strong enough. The rehabilitation period is just as important as having the cartilage removed. You must build up the thigh muscle, spend weeks with the physiotherapist. If I had been given £1 for every time I tightened my thigh and straightened my leg I would be a millionaire!

My biggest regret is that I stupidly delayed an operation after tearing a cartilage against West Ham during the 1977 Christmas holiday programme. I knew it was cartilage trouble the moment my knee began to click; exactly the same thing had happened to me three years earlier during a match for Newcastle at Birmingham. I told Arsenal I should have the cartilage taken out but they were short of first team players and asked me to carry on. I reluctantly decided to help them out and paid the price. I was not fully fit for the rest of the season, even playing at Wembley against Ipswich in the 1978 FA Cup Final. I think my leg locked about twenty times during the game. It had been a senseless decision to try and battle on. If I had gone straight into hospital after the West Ham match Arsenal would have had me back, fully fit, by March.

I had the cartilage removed at Nuffield Hospital, Marble Arch, after the Cup Final and that was the start of my problems. During the third game of the new season, a disastrous League Cup defeat at Rotherham, my knee, the left one this time, locked and blew up. Much to the delight of the partisan Yorkshire crowd, I was carried off by Fred Street and Don Howe. 'You will do anything not to take the blame, Macdonald', the crowd screamed their allegations. If only they could have felt the pain! Another op and this time the recovery was slow and full of problems. I fought my way back once more but was not happy. I had fluid removed by the syringe-full, X-rays that were always clear, and Nigel Harris said: 'This is ridiculous. I tidied your knee up the last time, there is nothing obviously wrong with it.' As a last resort I was sent for an arthrogram. My knee was injected with dye, blown up like a small football and pulled apart by a specialist called Bram Stoker. I relay this saga of injuries because at the time it was the most important few weeks of my life. I seemed to go from specialist to specialist, only to return home with the same answer for my wife Julie: 'They say there is nothing wrong'.

At last Nigel Harris spotted a tiny speck on yet another X-ray. 'Wait a minute, what the hell is that?' he asked. I couldn't see anything. 'It's just a piece of dust on the picture.' It turned out to be a small fragment of cartilage that a surgeon at Newcastle had left attached all those years ago. At the time it was the right decision, but a piece of gristle formed and floated about my knee until it got stuck in the joints. Harris promised nothing when he did the operation. 'No professional sportsman should have the same knee opened up three times', he told me. 'What I am doing is taking out a cartilage that shouldn't be there.'

That was my last time under the surgeon's knife. I fought like hell to play again and my hopes were high until Sweden. Now I am left with a rotten left knee and a slight but permanent limp. As a kid I had a pair of perfectly straight legs but years of tackles and operations has left me with a bow a cowboy would be proud of. People sometimes look at me in the street; I know what they are thinking: 'Hey, I know him, isn't that Malcolm Macdonald?'

People do forget quickly. I feel like an outsider at Highbury now. I have served my purpose. The players, too, are embarrassed. I am a mirror of their fears. Injury is the sportsman's biggest nightmare — no-one wants to be finished at 29.

2

Roy of the Rovers

I suffered my first setback at the age of fourteen when my dreams of becoming a professional footballer were shattered in one cruel letter from Chelsea Football Club. 'Sorry', it began, 'We think you are too small, come back when you are stronger. Build yourself up.' It was devastating reading and at the time I thought the bottom had fallen out of my world. The first setback is always the worst and I couldn't believe that anyone thought I was not good enough to make it.

I was only a kid and to be told I was too small made me depressed for weeks. Football meant everything to me; I had been trying desperately to be accepted by one of the local clubs and Chelsea were the first to answer. It just made me even more determined to prove them wrong. All through my life I have had more confidence in my ability than other people have. I can remember surprising my parents and masters at Queen's Manor School, Fulham, by passing my eleven-plus exam and I have shocked a lot of people in football since by getting to the top.

Football has always been in the Macdonald blood and from the moment my father, Charles, took me to watch Fulham at the age of three it was a certainty that I would keep the tradition going. My mother didn't worry about me going to Craven Cottage at such a young age, although her heart would have missed a beat if she had seen me passed over the heads of the men down to the other kids at the front of the terraces. She screamed in horror once when I came home with two black lines down my face, and my father had to explain they were only the impressions of the railings I had been peering through.

My father played for Hull City and Blyth Spartans and I think he was delighted that I showed an interest in his sport. Our semi-detached home in Finlay Street was only a goal kick from Craven Cottage and I was brought up on thirty-a-side matches in

Bishops Park and the excitement of watching the crowd on match days rushing past our front window.

I was a typical football-loving kid and put sport before anything else. Only two things got me up early in the morning, the day the old *Tiger* comic came through the letter box — Roy of the Rovers was my schoolboy hero — and when the Fulham players were training at Craven Cottage. If I knew Fulham were training I rushed down to carry their bags; Joe Buccuzi, Ian Black, Roy Dwight, even a fella called Jimmy Hill, they were all my heroes and I got to know them all. They knew me as the kid from up the road.

My first real idol was Johnny Haynes. I can see him now staring down from his famous Brylcreem advert. I was seven years old when I first saw him play and even then I could tell he was one of the greats. He was different from the rest, other players seemed to doff their cap to him and say: 'Here, John, you can have the ball, you can do more with it than me'.

He was rather like Liam Brady at Arsenal. How strange that a few years later I fell out with my idol and discovered what Johnny Haynes was really like.

It cost 6d to get into Craven Cottage those days and that was a small fortune for the local kids. By the end of the week our pockets were empty and it was a question of finding a hole in the fence or a friendly turnstile attendant. Once a few of us slipped into Chelsea by stepping over the railway track at the back of Stamford Bridge. A few days later we discovered that one of the lines was live!

The atmosphere was always good inside Stamford Bridge and Craven Cottage. The fans seemed to be a family; I can remember the white handkerchiefs being waved to catch the attention of the St John Ambulance man if someone had fainted. Alas, no such brotherly love to-day; the poor chap would probably be left or kicked by the thugs who use football grounds to relieve their frustration and bitterness.

I was a titch at school and began at outside left, probably because I could always sprint faster than anyone else. After passing my eleven-plus I was desperate to join St Clement Dancs School because they had the best football team in the area and won everything. I was speechless with rage when my parents told me I had to go to Sloane Grammar School, Chelsea. I was a very reluctant pupil on my first day, although eventually Sloane provided me with the sweetest moment of my school life. We beat Clement Danes in the London Grammar School Knockout trophy and I, now playing at centre half, scored the only goal of the game. It was a big shot clearance from my own half that bounced over the goalkeeper's head. They all count!

When I was twelve my father began to have health problems, and couldn't concentrate on his job as a painter and decorator. It put a lot of pressure on my mother, Florrie, who was left virtually single-handed to bring up four sons — me, David, Neil and James, who had only just been born. While Dad was in hospital mother did baby-minding for the local council to bring home a few more bob.

It was tough going and I didn't help her worries by getting into trouble at school. The headmaster complained that I paid too much attention to football and not enough to work. He was probably right, especially when carefully-drawn offside plans appeared in my maths homework book.

At fourteen I was the youngest boy to get into the school first team. Then suddenly I was dropped to concentrate on my studies. I was furious and had a terrible row with the games master, Mr Alford. But his hands had been tied; the order had come down from the top, Dr Henry: 'More work, less football for Macdonald'. I was relegated to the reserves and so hurt that I went out and scored four goals out of six in one of their rare matches.

Football had completely overtaken studies in my plans and there was only one thing I wanted to be. I was training two nights a week at Fulham and had a trial for London Grammar Schools.

Then Terry Casey, a former Irish amateur international and now head of coaching for the Lancashire Football Association, invited me to play for his club, Barnet. At fifteen I was left back in their Metropolitan League side and wanted to sign amateur forms. I felt good, I was proving Chelsea wrong.

Dear old Doctor Henry had other ideas, however, thought it was a terrible idea and refused to give me permission. So with all the arrogance in the world I quit school at the end of the next term. I found any job I could get my hands on. It was a fill-in between playing football and I started with stock-taking at the sports company of Alec Brook, the former British table tennis champion. The pay was only £9 10s a week but I was prepared to sacrifice anything to play football. I loved the football atmosphere at Barnet and mixing with fine players like Dennis Roach and Les Eason. I can remember the training sessions like yesterday, two hours of hard work, a hot shower and then a plate of beans on toast and a pint of milk.

My father died on Christmas Day 1966, when I was sixteen. My parents had already decided to move to the village of Forest Row in Sussex and take over a confectionery shop and it was therefore left to me, the eldest son, to run the business with my mother.

Suddenly I had more responsibilities than I thought possible, and my mother and I were two novices together. I was virtually thrown from school into dealing with company reps and at the start I was conned into buying things we were never even asked for. I was once left two dozen boxes of cigarettes that no-one wanted. The rep had told me they were the latest craze, but how can you sell a product that smells like cabbage? I was so furious about being conned that I smoked them all myself and kidded him next time that I had sold the lot.

I had to forget all about football to make a success of the business, and slowly my mother and I got the family back on its feet. It was very rewarding and looking back now, those months battling for survival pulled us all even closer together, and gave me a good early insight into business.

... Once the shop began showing a healthy profit I looked for a local club and my return to football came via the unlikely avenue of a driving instructor. He advised me to join Knowle Juniors in Sevenoaks, and then an old friend George Piper recommended me to Tonbridge in the Southern League. I played my first game for Tonbridge as an amateur in their reserve side in April 1967. I remember it so well because during the match my shorts split and fell to my ankles. What a start!

I really felt my career was lifting off again when, before the beginning of the new season, I was selected for three first team friendlies. We drew 2-2 with Barnsley, who included Paddy Howard, later to become a friend and team-mate at Newcastle and Arsenal, in their side, beat Fulham 2-1 and thrashed Brighton 4-1.

My first professional contract was £10 a week with £2 for a win and £1 for a draw plus travelling expenses. It worked out at about £17 a week and to me that was a fortune. I had arrived!

Harry Haslam was the Tonbridge manager and he insisted I play at right back in the first team. I had no ambitions yet to become a goalscorer, but right back was a joke position for me. I was left-footed, but Harry would just say: 'Son, I have never seen a left-sided player refuse to stand on his right leg. Get the No. 2 shirt on.' It was a nightmare and many times I kept moving inside before eventually ending up at outside left!

Then one day we were playing Hastings in the League, and 30 minutes before the kick-off Harry turned to me and said: 'Right, lad, put the No. 9 shirt on today'. Centre forward! I couldn't believe it. I had never played there before in my life and complained bitterly. But Harry had done his homework, he knew the Hastings centre half was slower than a carthorse and, using my speed, I managed to score a hat-trick.

I was on cloud nine when I got back into the dressing room. Three goals at seventeen in my first game at centre forward. Harry was waiting and I said: 'Not bad, Harry, you must give me the No. 9 from now on'. I boasted. 'You *might* get a blue one', came back the answer.

I got a blue one (the Tonbridge colours) all right — the No. 12 as Harry brought me down to earth by making me substitute. 'Don't get too cocky too soon, you are only a baby at this game.' It certainly taught me a lesson and gave me my first introduction to Harry Haslam's unique style of management and his own special sense of humour.

He has been taking the mickey out of me ever since, and poor Julie also took some terrible stick from him after the first time I took her to Tonbridge's ground, The Angel, on a wet Saturday afternoon. Julie's father was a trainer for her local club, East Grinstead, and she obviously thought that Tonbridge, like her Dad's team, played on the park with the spectators standing on planks of wood to keep their feet dry. When I called to take Julie to the game I couldn't believe it. She came to the door wrapped in jeans, anorak, scarf and wellington boots. I had forgotten to tell her that she would be sitting in the grand stand and all the other wives treated Saturday afternoon like a fashion parade. There was no time for her to change, Harry has reminded Julie of their first meeting ever since.

Harry was Mr Tonbridge in those days. He cut the grass, painted the lines, typed the letters and was the general dogs-body. I respected him for that and we have grown closer ever since. He has become a good friend of the family and advised me on each of my four transfers.

He gave me my first break in football and then at Fulham and Luton convinced others that I could become a goalscorer. He has driven me on throughout my career. I will always be indebted to Harry Haslam.

3

The reign of King John

When Harry Haslam left Tonbridge after eight years to become chief scout at Fulham, I suppose it was inevitable that I would follow him back to London. Harry obviously thought I had potential and, sure enough, two months later in August 1968 I walked past our old home in Finlay Street for a meeting with manager Bobby Robson.

Crystal Palace were also interested in signing me, but there was something unprofessional about Palace I didn't like. There seemed to be millions of players and only three teams; it was a scramble to find a coat peg, let alone get a game. And when Palace manager Bert Head offered me only £20 a week I made up my mind to join Fulham.

Robson was obviously reluctant to sign an eighteen-year-old full back with no League experience. 'I have not seen you play and, quite frankly, I'm taking a gamble', he told me. He finally offered me the same money as Head with a promise to renew my contract at the end of the season if things went well. It didn't look as though I was going to get more than £20 a week anywhere, so I decided to join Fulham. After all they were my team and all my mates still lived locally. And I liked Robson. He seemed an open, honest manager.

Fulham made a disastrous start, struggling against a crippling list of injuries and an inability to score goals. The reserve strikers were promoted and Haslam persuaded Robson to play me up front in the second team. I responded by scoring five goals in my first five matches. On 28 August I made my League debut at Oxford. I had two goals disallowed for offside, missed a sitter and we lost 1-0. It meant that Fulham had gone 690 minutes without a goal and the situation was desperate to say the least.

The following Friday we played Crystal Palace in a London derby under floodlights. There was a big crowd and the atmosphere inside the ground was one of hope, not for a win, but for a goal. Early in the first half a long clearance from goalkeeper Ian Seymour fell to me and I raced past Palace centre half John McCormick. I thought I was going too wide to get in a shot but managed to cut inside goalkeeper John Jackson and slip the ball into the net. As I turned away in celebration I saw Freddie Bush, a good friend of my father's, who was standing behind the goal. He had his fist raised high and was shouting 'That's my boy!' I can still see the joy on his face to-day. That goal meant so much to him and it brought home to me how much one goal can change a supporter's life for a day. We should have scored ten against Palace and I know I missed five.

Everyone started to tell me about the art of playing centre forward. In my naivety I would just say to them: 'I'm sticking the ball in the net, what is the problem?' I can remember playing for the first time with Frank Large, a big awkward striker who must have been a defender's nightmare. 'What's the plan, Frank?' I said as we ran out. 'If you see the onion bag', came the reply, 'give the ball a good leather.'

My joy of playing and scoring for Fulham was shattered by the sudden realization that I was only receiving the ball from certain members of the team. There were two cliques in the Fulham side, the Johnny Haynes crowd and the rest. It seemed as if players like Les Barrett, Jim Conway, Steve Earle and Fred Callaghan all played by kind permission of King John. The others went alone. Haynes would give a twenty-yard pass and then run and take it off the same player. Then he would give his famous shoulder shrug if his orders were not carried out. It was crazy and ruined any chance we had of doing well.

If I scored it was completely by accident to the team's tactics because I was never put through. During a televised League match at home to Blackburn I put us 1-0 ahead by running on to a Haynes cross-shot and scoring. It was a good feeling, another goal and the chance to watch it with my family on the box later that night. As I was trotting back to the middle accepting the congratulations Haynes came over. I thought he was actually going to say well done; instead there was just a terse 'Why didn't you leave that shot alone, it was going in?' I couldn't believe it and was completely shattered. I got home in a filthy mood and just sat in front of the television all night waiting for my goal.

Bobby Robson was never given a chance to manage Fulham. He was overruled and overrun. Robson would give the team instructions in the dressing room, then as soon as we got out on the pitch Haynes would change them. It was a disgusting show by a man who had such a good reputation in the game and a big following of schoolboys. The split inside the first team squad was beyond repair; Haynes and his men would go for lunch to one restaurant and the others in a different direction.

My head spun with politics. I can remember driving to London from Forest Row one day asking myself: 'What have I let myself in for? If this is what football is like at the top, they can stick it.'

Even Robson's attempt to instil some discipline into the club failed, as players treated Craven Cottage like a holiday camp — a place for a laugh and a joke. They simply didn't care. It backfired one week, however, on centre half John Dempsey. There was a rule that if you were late for training you were fined ten shillings. It went up to £2 the next day, and a third late appearance in a week carried a punishment of a week's wages.

Dempsey arrived the first day waving a ten bob note in his hand shouting: 'Look lads, naughty me, I'm late'. The next day, in came John with a pound note in each hand and the same grin on his face. He left home on time the following day, but there was a traffic jam over Kew Bridge and our Eire international was never late again:

The Craven Cottage carnival was the worst possible start for other young players like Barry Salvage. Bobby Moss, David Moreline and Ian Seymour, who became a good friend and best man at my wedding. All we wanted to do was learn and play, but it was impossible.

I resented Haynes bitterly and it was a tragedy that fine young prospects should have had to play for a club run by one man, the wrong one. I wonder if they blame him for not allowing their careers to take off? I certainly do. Young players should always be able to look to the senior players for help.

Now I look back on that period at Craven Cottage I can't help feeling sorry for Haynes. He was Mr Fulham and there is no doubt that he loved the club and the people. It must have destroyed him to feel his career ending and to watch a new generation of players coming into the club to take over his team. I can't forgive him for the way he treated us but now, strangely, I understand. It was almost a form of jealousy as he reluctantly let his association slip.

When he was in the mood Haynes was one of the great players.

Fulham owe him a lot and I just wish he had accepted me and the other young players who were drafted into the team. I played in a number of matches with John but never felt we were on the same side.

Something had to snap and on one Monday afternoon Robson called me into his small office. There was deep concern in his face and he chose his words very carefully: 'You can obviously see what is going on at this club', he said, 'I have got to put a stop to it before Fulham goes under. On Saturday I am going to play all the kids. They are the future of this club.' It was a sensational move by the manager but as I left him sitting alone I wondered why he had told me and not the others. In my naivety I thought he might be considering making me captain — or was it just desperation and he needed someone to talk to? I still felt excited but worried what the club's reaction would be.

Two days later Bobby Robson was sacked. His last effort to turn Fulham into a properly run club had failed. Haslam and coach Roy McCrohan went with him and they drowned their bitterness together over large glasses of sherry at the local pub. It was a bad day for me and it turned into a nightmare when the players were told that Johnny Haynes was to take over as manager. The day before our next match, a difficult game at Preston, Haynes called me into that same small manager's office in the old Cottage. I was the team's top scorer but Haynes just said: 'You will not be in the side against Preston tomorrow, you will play for the reserves. While I am in control I don't want your type of player in my team.'

I hope today the men that backed Johnny Haynes in that week at Fulham now realize their mistake. They have only got to look at Robson's record at Ipswich to prove they were wrong. Robson was disgracefully treated; he didn't have a skeleton in the cupboard, he had one on the pitch, the powerful Haynes.

Before Robson left he had promised me a flat in Richmond at £4 a week. I desperately needed a home near the ground and went to confirm the arrangement with secretary Graham Hortop. After 24 hours of hurried talks I was told I couldn't have it, only to discover that Jim Conway moved in a week later. Haynes didn't talk to me once during his seventeen days in control and then Bill Dodgin took over. The club went from bad to diabolical. I was stuck at outside left when I got back in the team and received just four passes in one game — none from King John.

Fulham signed Cliff Jones from Tottenham and Brian Dear from West Ham. Dear got six goals in the last twelve matches but my five goals at the start of the season still made me second highest scorer. That meant a lot to me in my first season in League football. Those goals were the only thing I enjoyed in nine months of misery.

On Tuesday, 31 December 1968, Julie and I were married at St Swithun's Church, East Grinstead. Our first home was in Wimbledon; the cheapest flat I could find was £8 plus another £3 for electricity and gas. It meant that we survived on about £4 a week and I spent the next summer working in a local factory to bring home a few more pounds. It was hard going but we had our dreams. I can recall spending a few hours of our two-day honeymoon wandering around the Ideal Home Exhibition planning our first house.

Money doesn't seem to matter when you are single, as the world and its problems pass you by. To need money is another matter, and I was under a lot of strain when I went to see Dodgin and Hortop on the first day of training for the 1969-70 season. I had received no flat or salary increase as promised and my message to Fulham was simple: 'If you don't give me my deal I am walking out of football'.

A meeting with chairman Tommy Trinder didn't help. He invited Julie and me to his home for tea the next day but all he wanted to do was soften me up through her. My mind was made up and I wiped the smile off our comedian chairman's face with my next statement. 'Mr Trinder', I said, 'If Fulham force me to quit football I will do one thing before I leave.'

'What's that, Malcolm?' he asked warily.

'I will put Johnny Haynes up against a wall and smash his face in.'

That was my last meeting with anyone at Fulham. I meant what I said. I would have quit and gone into the insurance business — and made a better living. My determination clearly worked, as two days later Haynes actually spoke to me. 'There is some good news for you', he said, 'They want you in the offices.'

I thought my flat had come through but all Hortop told me to do was wait in a small office. And there I sat, waiting. For two hours I stayed in that office, not knowing what I was supposed to do or who, if anyone, was coming to see me. Suddenly the door flew open and in walked this dapper little man, immaculately dressed, shoes polished so you could see your face in them and a handkerchief flopping out of his top pocket. Close on his heels was Harry Haslam, no jacket and his hands and arms covered in car grease.

'I have had a bloody awful day', the little man said. 'I have come here to sign you. Oh yes, I'm Alec Stock from Luton.' It looked as though the only one who had suffered an awful day was Harry. I discovered later their car had broken down on the M1 and Harry had been left to fix it.

Alec put a blue form in front of me and added, 'Now you can either sign that or I'm going home for tea'. I took one look and signed. Luton had doubled my wages. Once again Harry had convinced his manager of my potential and Luton had paid £17,500 for me. Their original offer had been £12,500 but Fulham pushed up the price. It was a lot of money for someone who had only played eight League matches and scored five goals. I didn't realize, however, that Luton had signed me as a left back.

I immediately had tremendous respect for Alec Stock. I had never met a manager like him before. There was an air of authority about him. That respect lives on today; I have never met one man with so many admirers.

I was told to report to Kenilworth Road at ten o'clock the next day, and with that Stock left with Harry, sticking up his greasy thumb at me, again not far behind.

Although Fulham were my club I had no regrets about leaving them behind. I saw no future for me at Craven Cottage, the manager clearly didn't rate me and Haynes was still around. It is ironic therefore that I should eventually go back as commercial executive soon after being forced to quit football.

As a player I found them unprofessional, the music hall joke, but today under the guidance of chairman Ernie Clay, they are a football club again. My job is to sell Fulham FC and I have great ambitions for the ground where I watched my first football. Our biggest project is to turn Craven Cottage into the first all-seater stadium in England.

As I walked away from the Cottage for the last time as a player with them on that warm July evening I suddenly realized that I had signed without even telling Julie. Would she want to live in Bedfordshire? Where do Luton play, anyway? I asked myself.

She was just about to inquire if there was any news of our Fulham flat when I told her: 'By the way, I signed for Luton this afternoon'.

'Who?'

4

The Mad Hatter

It was Friday 8 August 1969 when I first realized that I could become a successful goalscorer. There were 24 hours to go before my Luton debut against Barrow and Alec Stock was in the middle of his last team talk.

'Gentlemen', he had begun. 'We are going to win promotion from the Third Division this season. And this is how. We must not lose more than eight matches in the next nine months, we need at least 80 goals and can't afford to concede more than 32. It is as simple as that.' Dear old Alec had it all worked out and scribbled down on paper. Then he started to give each player a goal target.

We all laughed as centre half Terry Branston was told he must score five and laid bets against full back Jack Bannister reaching his target of three. Laurie Sheffield, my partner up front, was sitting next to me and seemed happy with the eighteen goals Alec told him to score. I thought I could get about the same when Alec turned to me and said, 'You, Malcolm, will score me 30'. My mouth dropped open in disbelief.

Alec had signed me as a full back and yet suddenly he wanted me to get 30 goals. All the other players sitting around the dressing room just stared at me, they obviously didn't believe I could get them either. It was Graham French who broke the silence when he said: 'I don't know what you are worrying about, Malcolm, if you can't score 30 goals in a season from all the chances I make you shouldn't be playing'.

The more I thought about Alec's target the more determined I became to meet it. I had always loved the excitement of scoring goals, even going back to my school days and the Tonbridge hat-trick as an emergency centre forward. 'Alec Stock wants me to score 30 goals this season', I told Julie that night. 'I'm going to become a great striker.' I went to sleep dreaming of goals, scoring against Barrow, getting the cup final winner at Wembley, playing for England ... I don't think Alec realized exactly what he had stirred up inside me with his demand.

We beat Barrow 3-0 and I didn't score. I was pleased about getting two points but bitterly disappointed not to reduce my target. In midweek we beat Bournemouth and I got the only goal of the game. I can remember coming off afterwards and thinking: 'Only 29 to go'. I don't know whether Alec was playing a psychological game with us but it worked. Every player wanted to reach his goal and it kept morale high even in defeat. At the end of the season the manager's sums incredibly almost came true; we got promotion and I scored 27 goals. I was delighted and felt excited about what the future held for me.

I loved it at Luton. From the moment I had to cash a £2 cheque for the train fare on my first day and buy a street map to find Kenilworth Road I was a real Mad Hatter. It was probably because the atmosphere was in such contrast to Fulham but Luton was one big happy family. And sitting at the top was Alec Stock. He commanded respect. Alec was the boss and everyone knew it, from the groundsman to the secretary. I regard myself very lucky to have played under a man who I believe is one of the great managers.

Stock mixed fun with football and will go down in history as the man with the magic wand. He has turned small clubs into giants, ordinary players into good ones, and stars into internationals. I can see him now, standing at the front of the coach after an away win and bursting into song. 'When you're winning' he would sing and everyone had to join in! Even the chairman.

We lived at 95 Oak Road, a little terraced house that backed onto the football ground. I would open the front door on match days and join the crowd going to the game. 'Hello Mac, how many goals is it going to be today? what's their centre half like? how did you miss that sitter last week?' The fans liked me and for the first time I struck up a relationship with my supporters.

There is no doubt that football crowds need a hero, an idol, someone to pin their hopes on. That man is usually the goalscorer, the No. 9. Everything else in a game is often forgotten if the centre forward scores a last-minute winning goal. It is he who accepts the praise of the fans, the thanks of his team-mates and the headlines the next morning. In contrast, of course, the goalscorer carries the can if things go wrong.

I believe it is the most exciting role in football. A death or glory job. I just can't understand why there is such a shortage of good goalscorers around to-day. When I was a kid everyone wanted to be the centre forward, we would take it in turns to play in attack. Surely times have not changed so much in the last 15 years? A new Jimmy Greaves must be out there somewhere.

Luton only stumbled across Malcolm Macdonald the goalscorer by accident. We played the Italian Under 21 team during the build-up to my first season and I was told to play at left back in the first half before senior choice Jack Bannister took over. Early in the game Mike Harrison, the former Chelsea winger, pulled a thigh muscle and at half time I was switched to outside left. Nothing was said to me after the game and it was only before my debut against Barrow that Alec revealed how highly he rated me.

It was Harry Haslam again who had faith in my ability. He had already persuaded Bobby Robson to sign me for Fulham and then convinced him to play me as an emergency striker. Now he had assured Alec that I would score goals for Luton.

I began to learn the trade of a goalscorer although I was always pig-headed. I wasn't really interested in diagonal runs and running off the ball. I just wanted to be put through and score. The coaches would scream for the diagonal run. But all that went through my mind was 'Get it, turn and shoot'. They would just shake their heads in frustration.

Luton owned a small shop in Oak Road and every afternoon I went into a back room with a Johnny Giles signed plastic football. For hours I did the same thing, I would trap the ball as it bounced off one wall, turn and shoot. It was the only time I got near to Johnny Giles throughout my career!

The other players, as well as first team coach Jimmy Andrews, would throw their arms up in disbelief during a game as I crashed away at all angles. If I saw the goal I shot. I must have been terrible to involve in a team plan. Matt Tees would play his role up front by the book while all I was interested in doing was putting the ball in the onion bag.

In the end they just accepted me as a goalscorer and let me get on with it. I would miss three, perhaps score one, then get a hat-trick and just keep ploughing on. Luton skipper Mike Keen once said to me during a game: 'Don't worry if you miss, just keep having a go. You will score eventually and their defence is scared stiff of you.' Keen was a good player and the first to understand that I liked the ball knocked through on a straight run. Terry

Hibbitt and I had a superb understanding during great days at Newcastle, and Alan Ball and Liam Brady and I were on the same wavelength at Arsenal.

My motto about goalscoring and what I believe has been the secret of my success is that I have never been afraid to miss. A supporter said to me after I retired: 'I didn't realize just how many goals you scored in your career'. I was flattered but replied, 'Fella, you couldn't count the ones I have missed'.

There were some amazing characters in the Luton side that won promotion to the Second Division and then battled to give Alec Stock what he desperately wanted, a team in the First. Graham French was a poor man's George Best. He had all Best's problems but not the publicity.

The one story that emphasizes French's lifestyle came when we were playing away to Bury and all the players had to report to Luton Station early on Saturday morning. Alec, superbly dressed as usual, carried out a roll call and we were one short. French was late. The British Rail authorities were keen to get the special train out of the station, but Alec would not budge until French arrived. He was a very valuable member of the team. As the manager paced up and down the platform, I saw Graham staggering towards us in the other direction. He was blind drunk and wanted to tell the world what a great all-night party he had been to. Somehow we kept him away from Alec and convinced our left winger that sleep and not another vodka and tonic was his best pre-match build up.

He slept the entire journey and again in the dressing room before the match. We eventually woke him up at 2.30 and said: 'You must get changed now, Graham, we are going out soon'.

French was brilliant from the kick-off. He went past the Bury full back as if he wasn't there and made two goals for Matt Tees and me before Bury knew what had hit them. All we did was give the ball to French and wait for the cross.

As French received another pass on the half-way line he suddenly stopped, put his foot on the ball and said, 'Look, I have been up all night, and I'm shattered. Why do you keep giving me the ball? I don't want it. I just want to sleep.' And with that he limped off. To this day I don't know if Alec knew how bad Frenchy really was.

Alec, however, always stuck by his players. He was tremendously loyal inside and out of the club. After French was involved in a shooting incident at a Luton pub and was sent to prison, he one day received a parcel and inside was the complete Luton Town strip and this message from Alec: 'We haven't changed but you have got to. Look forward to seeing you.' That just proves what a big man Alec Stock is.

It is difficult for me not to always mention Alec when I talk about my happy years at Luton. From the little painted wooden men he used when discussing the opposition to words in the dressing room like: 'It is a lovely day, gentlemen, I think we can do a little bit this afternoon', he was different.

He once called me into his office and produced a big blue leather-bound book that contained every detail possible of all the players Alec had been involved with. He had logged out the history of teams, how many goals a player should score, the strengths of certain players, the points needed to win championships, the points a team must get to stay up and lots more. Alec's life history in football was in that book and to my knowledge it is still being added to today.

Newspapers began to speculate how much I was worth on the transfer market and I began to wonder if I could make it right to the top. The rumours didn't unsettle me and I was rather impressed that big clubs were being linked. I wanted to find out what the future held for Malcolm Macdonald.

Alec had built a good team but we were not going to win promotion to the First Division and then towards the end of the 1970-71 season Luton were suddenly under financial pressure. Vehicle and General, the insurance company of our chairman Tony Hunt, went bust and I was obviously the club's hottest property on the transfer market if Luton suddenly needed some quick money.

It was one day in April when Alec took me to one side during training and said: 'I'm going to have to sell you'. I was sad to leave Luton but ready to further my education. If Luton had been promoted that season, however, I don't think I would have wanted to play in the First Division for anyone else.

We were playing Cardiff the next day and had to win by two clear goals to get into next season's Watney Cup, a competition for the League's highest scorers. 'Joe Harvey of Newcastle is interested and will be in the stand', Alec said. 'It's up to you now, you have got to do the business.' We won 3-0 and I got them all. Alec told me to report to the Kenilworth Road offices in the morning and overnight I discovered that Manchester United, who had first option on me, were not interested but Chelsea, the club that turned me down as a kid, were keen.

I waited two hours for Alec the next morning, just sitting in his office waiting for something to happen. It was a repeat of my experience at Fulham two years earlier when once again I waited for Alec to put me out of my misery. The door burst open and this time it was Alec who was hot and bothered. 'I have done the deal', he said. 'This is the fee, this is what you will get and Joe Harvey is waiting for you in the Great Northern Hotel in London.' While I had been waiting, Alec had driven down the M1, done the business and sped back again!

I motored down to London with Haslam without knowing what to expect. I was excited at the thought of playing in the First Division and, after 49 goals in 88 League matches and nine Cup goals for Luton, knew I was ready. After day-long talks with Joe Harvey I signed for Newcastle and once again I had joined a club I knew nothing about. But it wasn't a gamble, I was sure of that.

The day was almost ruined on the return journey when a lorry on the M1 threw up something and smashed the windscreen of my Opel car. Harry, who was sitting in the passenger's seat, was showered with glass and for one ghastly moment I thought he had lost the sight of an eye. We raced to Harry's home and his wife Trudy got the splinter of glass out before any permanent damage had been caused.

· It was the second time I had suffered a smashed windscreen accident on the motorway. A few months earlier when I was returning from Watford a nutcase with an air rifle decided to use cars as target practice. The repair company found pellets embedded in the back seat and headlamp!

The long talks with Joe Harvey and drama of the accident to Harry had made me forget that it was 7 May, Julie's 21st birthday. I didn't even have a card to give her, only my late arrival and the news that we were off once more on a journey into the unknown. To Newcastle.

Julie wasn't really impressed. After all, 21st birthdays are something special. So Alan Owen, a good friend who had been helping Julie answer the telephone and turning reporters away from the front door, and I decided to at least end the day in style with a bottle of champagne and a take-away meal. We chose steaks and Julie wanted her favourite food, scampi.

Alan had just joked 'We have got some scampi for the cat' when Julie opened her package to find three tiny bits of scampi. She went berserk and screamed at me: 'You didn't remember my birthday and now this. I have had a terrible day and it's all your fault. You're thoughtless ....'

I sat there, helpless, thinking to myself, 'I have just signed for a big First Division club and this should be one of the happiest days of my life. Instead everything has gone wrong from the moment I put pen to paper.

'Have I done the wrong thing? Life was so good at Luton.'

5

Goals to Newcastle

Joe Harvey had a reputation for coming straight to the point and our first meeting was no exception. 'So you're the little so-and-so who has just cost me another £30,000', he said before we had even shaken hands.

It was the start of a good relationship I had with Joe. I respected him and he believed in me; we were a good team. Between us I think we did a lot for Newcastle and loved every minute of it. Some people said that Joe Harvey had black and white blood, such was his commitment to the North East.

Our first meeting in Joe's bedroom in the Great Northern Hotel (how ironical that it should be the same hotel where my parents spent their honeymoon) followed a great example of Alec Stock's shrewd business brain. The clubs had agreed a fee of £150,000 but overnight the price increased and my hat-trick cost Newcastle £10,000 a goal. 'Sign this quickly before the price goes up again', Harvey added. And he shoved a contract under my nose.

So for the second time I joined a club that was a mystery to me. Newcastle, of course, were a big name and I had no hesitation in signing for them. But it was impossible at that stage to gauge the fervour of football in the North East or the adulation they give to their successful players. Even now when I talk to people about life being so different in Newcastle I am sure they don't really understand.

It is impossible to appreciate the passion and pride football generates at St James' Park until you have actually lived through it. The Newcastle people treated me like a king and they will always have a special corner in my memories.

I was the classic case of the Southern boy trying to establish fame and fortune in the North and decided to make an immediate impact. I hired a sparkling new limousine for the day and asked a friend, complete with peaked cap, to chauffeur me up for my opening day in the First Division.

It sounds corny now but I wanted to throw everything into that transfer. It was vital that I made a success of the next few years. I couldn't believe the reception waiting for me at St James' Park. Joe, club officials, the press and supporters were all at the main entrance. My pal played his part superbly, opening the door for me and asking the crowd to stand back.

As I stepped out, a broad North East accent somewhere in the crowd said: 'He must be the only player to arrive in his signing-on fee'. It was the voice of Bob Cass, *The Sun* newspaper's football man in the North East, and one of the great characters I met in Newcastle. His joke broke the ice and a day I secretly feared turned into the start of my most successful playing days.

Now I have retired I look back on my five seasons at Newcastle as the peak of my career. I hit a level of goalscoring consistency that was not bettered by anyone in the country and won all my fourteen England caps while at St James' Park. I am proud of my First Division record of 59 goals in 187 matches. Newcastle were not the best team in the country but on our day we could beat anyone.

I am sure I could have struck that kind of form for Arsenal if I had played longer under the influence of coach Don Howe. It is one of my biggest disappointments that just as Arsenal matured again along with gifted players like Liam Brady and Graham Rix my left knee packed up for good.

My first season for Newcastle began with a 2-0 defeat at Crystal Palace and a 0-0 draw at Tottenham that was famous for a number of stupid bookings at the start of the now famous referees' clampdown. Spurs Eire international full back Joe Kinnear was cautioned for handball as he caught the ball going out of play for a throw-in to his side. It was that kind of referee.

The disappointment of only one point from our first two matches was forgotten when I made my home debut against Liverpool. I had never experienced anything like it before, there was a 45,000 capacity crowd locked inside St James' Park and thousands more trying to get in. It was my introduction to Geordie fever and the atmosphere was electric. Nerves were growing in my stomach as I got changed and I looked around at the more experienced players in our side, men like Bobby Moncur and Frank Clark, and they didn't seem to be bothered at all. Was it like this every home game?

I desperately wanted to score and it was beyond my wildest dreams that I would get a hat-trick in our 3-2 win. I made it 1-1 from the penalty spot after David Young had been brought down. It was 2-1 when I turned quickly and shot across Ray Clemence into the top corner. That remains one of the best goals I have scored and as the ball went in my old Luton saying flashed through my mind: 'Get it, turn and shoot'. Good old Johnny Giles. John Tudor, my good friend and partner up front, slipped me through the Liverpool defence for my third.

The scenes that followed are still some of the wildest I have ever been involved with. Hundreds of fans came on to chair me back to the middle and from that moment the Geordies adopted me as SuperMac. For the rest of the game they sang: 'SuperMac, Superstar, how many goals have you scored so far?' The papers the next morning were full of my new nickname and, after just two years as a striker, I was an idol. It was a fairy tale and I was happy playing the leading role.

The last thing I remember about my home debut was charging through the Liverpool defence in search of a fourth goal. I was about to flick the ball wide of Clemence when he caught me in the face with his left boot. Goodnight! I was then convinced I was at home in bed, dreaming of my Newcastle debut. I saw a face and thought it was Julie. 'Darling', I said. 'I'm going to score a hat-trick today.' The reply brought me back to reality: 'Shut up you Southern idiot, you just have'. It was my best pal Frank Clark who had come in to see how I was.

Apparently I had been helped off by our coach Keith Burkinshaw suffering from concussion and face cuts. I have still got a scarred upper lip to prove it.

The atmosphere never dropped that season and every game was like a cup final. At Anfield I decided to get my own back on Clemence. I admit that when I ran out in front of the Kop revenge was on my mind.

My chance came early on when Clemence went up for a cross. As he gathered the ball and dropped to the ground I went in. It was not a dirty foul but I did catch him. On reflection it was stupid because had I gone only for the ball there was a chance I might have scored. No sooner had I made contact with the Liverpool goalkeeper than a fist hit me in the side of the throat. I looked up to see Tommy Smith standing over me: 'The next time I'll break your back', he snarled. It was the start of a running feud I had with Smith, on and off the pitch.

The more goals I scored, the more publicity I got. Television, radio, newspapers, advertising companies all wanted me for different projects and I obliged. I enjoyed it and I knew the Geordies expected me to. They have been brought up on goalscoring centre forwards and I was their new hero. Joe Harvey knew how much his players meant to the public. He would send us out to functions because it was good for the image of the club. Even on Thursday night Joe would say: 'Go for a couple of hours, have a few halves and talk to the people'.

With publicity of course comes jealousy and it was inevitable that I would upset people with my comments. I have said many controversial things in my career but they have always been honest. I have never gone out of my way to instigate a row or upset another player or manager. I once received a parcel with a Liverpool date stamp on it and thought someone had sent me a present or perhaps a book to sign. Inside there was just a neatly wrapped house brick inside with a message tied around the middle. 'We don't think you're a brick', it said. 'Just as thick as it.' It had cost them £1 to send.

Joe Harvey was a real players' manager; laughing at the moaners, encouraging the worried and offering Terry Hibbitt a cigarette on Friday morning when he complained about his crib hand at the local the night before. I never had to ask for a raise in four seasons at Newcastle; Joe would just come up and say: 'I got you a few more bob today, Mal' and there it would be in the next pay packet.

Harvey, who always left the tactics to Keith Burkinshaw, once gave the best pre-match team talk I have experienced. We were in Italy for the Anglo-Italian Cup Final against Fiorentina and the running of the side was completely in Joe's hands because Burkinshaw was involved in a wages dispute with Newcastle.

We hadn't seen Joe at all on the day of the game when, with fifteen minutes left to kick off, he stormed into the dressing room. 'Right, you bastards', he said, 'I have been involved with this club for years as a player, captain, coach and manager and have never lost a Cup Final.

'So I don't want you lot spoiling my record — go out and beat these Italians.' How could we let him down after that?

That talk was typical of Harvey's attitude to the game. He was not the best manager in the business but he was a fighter. The public knew he gave 24 hours a day for Newcastle United Football Club and the players never let him down. I never played in a game when the entire team didn't give their all for Joe Harvey.

At the height of my career at Newcastle I was involved in one of the most worrying incidents of my life. In this age of violence, bomb warnings and death threats seem to be accepted by the British public as a way of life. Believe me, when it happens to you it is a terrifying experience. About 24 hours before an important home game an Irish voice telephoned St James' Park to say I would be shot on Saturday afternoon.

I knew nothing about the phone call until I arrived home on Friday afternoon to discover two burly policemen waiting for me. At first I didn't want to take it seriously, but they convinced me I could be in danger. One of them kept watch all night and the other stayed inside our Morpeth home. It was not the ideal build-up to a match but I was grateful for the security they installed for me. We had breakfast together, travelled to the ground in the same car and they escorted me from the car park to the dressing rooms.

I was not allowed to stop to sign autographs and a number of children were knocked aside (I hope they understand now). My two new friends checked my dressing room locker and even stood outside the toilet! When we went into the tunnel my bodyguards came too. 'You're not playing as well, fellas, are you?' I joked. It was the same at half time, a big bobby either side to escort me back into the changing room.

It sounds now as if they were taking their responsibilities too far but their job was my safety and if anything had happened they would have been to blame. At the end of the match they just said: 'That's it, you're safe now' and went their separate ways. Suddenly I didn't feel safe and spent the rest of the night peering around corners and being suspicious of any strange face.

The premature break-up of Joe Harvey's Newcastle team and the end of the happiest years of my playing life came in 1975. It began with a small incident and just kept snowballing.

Frank Clark, who was discussing a new contract with the club, was suddenly asked to play right back in a home match against Birmingham. That was unheard-of. There was only one position Frank could play, left back. He was Mr Consistency, one of the best No. 3s I have played with and I have seen only one man skin Clarky — Leicester's Keith Weller.

We lost 2-1 against Birmingham and thirty minutes after the game Harvey came out of a meeting with the directors to tell

Frank: 'Sorry, there is no new contract, the club are giving you a free transfer'. As far as I was concerned that was a board decision and the break-up had begun.

The next bombshell was that Joe Harvey was asked to resign. It was more like kicked out. The club clearly had plans for big changes although no-one knew what they were. Players began to leave, Keith Burkinshaw went to Tottenham and Harvey parted company. 'What is happening to our club?' I can remember asking the rest of the players before one training session.

The Newcastle public are still waiting for the glory days to return. They will get their wish one day because Newcastle are too big to be second best for long. They are a sleeping giant that needs shaking and injecting with new life.

We gave the Geordies something to celebrate but only touched on the potential that is lying dormant at St James' Park. It will remain one of the mysteries of football why Newcastle United are not paired today with the greats. They should be.

6

No Lee-way

Newcastle United needed a big man to replace Joe Harvey. The players, the public, the entire club needed a figurehead, someone to light a fire under the potential and keep it burning. Newcastle United didn't need Gordon Lee.

I was playing in South Africa during the summer of 1975 when Newcastle announced their new manager, and a local journalist, John Gibson, rang me to ask who I thought had got the job. I knew who I wanted. 'Jack Charlton, Cloughie?' I said. 'No, Gordon Lee.' ... Who? ...

The name didn't mean much to me although I discovered later that he had a reputation as a disciplinarian and his record at Blackburn was good. But was he big enough, good enough to take on Newcastle as his first job in the First Division?

There was worse to come from Gibson's phone call. 'Lee says there will be no stars at St James' Park. He doesn't want any one player treated like an idol.' That was bad news for me and Lee's first big mistake. In my opinion the Newcastle public need a hero, a man they can identify with. Why did Lee want to change that even before he had tasted the unique atmosphere?

Lee's appointment worried me but I was prepared to admit I was wrong and on my first day back hoped I would be pleasantly surprised after a meeting with our new leader. After a few minutes all my fears were justified.

His first words to me were: 'Tell me about Terry Hibbitt, I understand he is a trouble-maker?' I couldn't believe my ears. All I wanted was a get-to-know-you talk and suddenly I was in the middle of an inquiry. I just said: 'Mr Lee, you had better find out yourself' and walked out.

I don't know whether Gordon Lee was under orders to upset players or break up the team but he certainly succeeded. Terry Hibbitt did whine and groan about things but the balance of his contribution to the team weighed in his favour. He was a great player. If he started to moan on the pitch you just told him to belt up and reminded him that he was playing well.

I knew from our first meeting that Gordon Lee and I were not going to see eye to eye. We never hit it off and were not on the same wavelength. It was a pity because I had been prepared to battle for Newcastle alongside the new manager. By the end of the season all the fight had gone out of me.

In the beginning I couldn't work out whether Gordon Lee was being serious or just playing games. The training sessions were a joke. Some of the funniest moments of my life were spent with Lee and his ball tricks.

He once asked us to split into teams and hop towards the goal, left hand on our hip and the other hand holding the ball above our head. We then had to throw the ball against the bar and hop back again. Now does that sound like hard pre-season training? It took me back to my early school days when we had a lady teacher for physical education.

Lee then appeared with a huge bag of balls and said: 'Right, lads, we are going to concentrate on tactics today'. He took a ball out and proceeded to take a throw-in. 'When you take a throw-in you must keep both feet on the ground.' That was too much for me and I just burst out laughing while the other players watched open-mouthed.

Lee came over and screamed at me: 'You have no right to be a professional footballer. You never take anything seriously.' He was right, I couldn't take this seriously. I was struggling to get a sweat on, let alone prepare for the new season. He appointed Richard Dinnis as his number two and the coaching went from bad to worse.

The split between Lee and me grew with every incident. I did an advertisement for Tartan Beer along with a number of players throughout the country. They called it McTartan Bitter but Lee didn't like the image it gave footballers. 'I don't like professionals advertising drink', he said. I couldn't see the harm in it, everyone knows that players like a pint after a game.

I didn't think much of his image either after an amazing scene one day in the Derby dressing room. Micky Burns had been sent off early in the game and we fought like mad to stay in the match with Terry Hibbitt doing the job of two men in midfield. Hibbitt had a magnificent game and it was no fault of his that we lost 3-2.

Terry and I were last out of the bath and all the kit had been packed away except a pair of boots sitting on top of the skip in a brown paper parcel. 'Hello, who is leaving?' joked Terry. 'You are' came back the sharp reply from Lee. 'Freddie Goodwin of Birmingham is waiting to speak to you.' It was a disgraceful piece of man-management. Terry had been brilliant but he did not get one word of praise from the manager, or warning about any transfer talks that day.

That was enough for me and I soon made it clear that I didn't want to play for Lee again when my contract expired at the end of the season. Things were happening that saddened and confused me. I have never been one for getting involved with cliques but suddenly we had a players' committee, small meetings in locked rooms and a lot of gossip running through the club.

I like an open-house atmosphere. The more the merrier has always been my motto and it seemed to worry Lee that I didn't react to what was going on at St James' Park. I believe he was jealous of me during those months. He was jealous of the relationship I had with the Newcastle public.

He brought in Alan Gowling as my new strike partner and although Alan did well and scored a lot of goals, he didn't get the same publicity as me. I would be asked by the media to comment all the time on incidents, which only drove the wedge deeper into the split between me and Gordon Lee and Newcastle. Lee once said about me: 'I will not talk about him, I will only talk about players'. Charming!

It was clear that the best thing for both of us was if I left and it flared to a head after we had been murdered 5-0 at Wolves. We conceded four goals in the second half and the ball hardly crossed the halfway line as Wolves drove forward. We gave away silly goals and Alan Kennedy, our young left back who has now matured into one of the best in the country at Liverpool, was responsible for at least three of them. He needed to be told what he was doing wrong but in the dressing room after the game nothing was said, Alan was just left to make the same mistakes again.

I decided to offer him some advice and no sooner had I started when Dinnis screamed across the dressing room at me: '*You* advise? *You* have done nothing in this game except stand on the halfway line. You haven't helped the team one little bit.' That was like a red rag to a bull for me and all the bitterness of the previous months spilled out. The dressing room was not the best place to have a row but things needed to be said.

'You can't speak to me like that', I shouted at Dinnis. 'You have offered nothing to this club, nor has he', pointing at Lee as he ducked into the toilet away from the bullets. There was no stopping me now. 'You're supposed to be the coach, well, coach Alan Kennedy. He could be a great player with some help. It is about time we heard you. All you do is carry the balls around.'

It eventually died down and everyone was left to his thoughts. I firmly believe that you must give a striker his head, let him do his own thing on some occasions. It may sound arrogant but I always knew I would score goals. There are days when a forward is going to struggle; those are not the days to criticize him and call him names. There might be twelve games a season when a goalscorer looks the worst player on the pitch. That doesn't make him a bad player and I have watched a dozen 5-0 defeats from the halfway line.

It is a different life in defence. Four players are working as a team usually against three, covering for each other. There is no reason why mistakes should be made. Up front it is lonely, you are often left to fight it out against four, perhaps with occasional support. You have got to make your own chances and sometimes they don't come or the goalkeeper makes a great save from the one opening you get all afternoon. That is how small the dividing line is between failure and success as a goalscorer. It doesn't make you a bad player; how many times did Jimmy Greaves only come to life in the last minute to score the winning goal?

Another of Lee's annoying habits was criticizing players in the newspapers and mentioning things you knew nothing about. At one stage we were lacking so much in midfield I began dropping back to try and help out. I hadn't been told and it was just reacting to our needs. Lee was asked why I was playing so deep and I read the next morning: 'We are working on a new plan for Malcolm'. So the next game I stayed up front in my old position. He didn't say anything.

I am the world's worst spectator when I am injured and didn't like what I saw during a home game against Wolves. We were not in the same class as Wolves in the first half, lucky to be only one goal down, and from my seat there were a million things wrong with our performance. I decided to go to the dressing room to offer some advice and couldn't believe my ears when I pushed through the door. Lee was saying: 'It's going great, lads, don't worry, you are doing fabulous'. I looked at the players and the expressions on their faces. They knew they were getting murdered.

Before I got back to my seat Newcastle had equalized and they went on to win 5-1. It was one of the most amazing comebacks I have seen and nothing will ever convince me that what Gordon Lee said at half time made any difference. The next day I read how Lee had told the players where they were going wrong at half time. 'I tore into them', he said.

By the end of the 1975-76 season the split was beyond repair and my love affair with Newcastle was over. I needed a new challenge and couldn't raise my game for Gordon Lee. It was a very important period of my career and I didn't want it ruined. I was the most consistent goalscorer in the country and I had more ambitions to fulfil.

My contract had expired but Newcastle, so the small print said, held a year's option. I decided to fight that in a bid to get away and it was at this stage that I wrote two letters to Newcastle chairman Lord Westwood, legally challenging the club's right to hold me to that option. I didn't receive any reply and the only conversation I had regarding my plans were three anonymous phone calls warning me not to go ahead. To this day I don't know who they were from or why I received them but I do know I would have gone to court.

I had legal advice and financial backing to smash that clause and such was my determination I would have quit football if I had lost. As I said in the introduction to this book, I feel very bitter about the way players are treated in England. I explain why in Chapter 18.

Such was the newspaper coverage of my disenchantment with Newcastle (I had refused to train when the players reported back for the 1976-77 season) that the entire world seemed to know I was keen to get away.

It was not long before I received the first of the naughty phone calls a player gets when he is wanted by another club. It is called 'tapping' and I call them naughty because, in football law, they are illegal. Everyone knows they go on, but they are still illegal.

They are phone calls made by a middleman, or a friend of the interested manager to a player under contract. 'Would you be keen on joining so and so?' you are asked. 'What would the fee be, how much do you want, can you put a bit of pressure on your end?' If you show interest, the middleman — you often never get to meet him — reports back and the buying club put the bid in knowing you are keen to move.

Tapping will always go on, so why not make it legal? It would stop all these underhand deals and ridiculous situations when the player and manager know what is going on but never actually get round to talking about it. The players must be delighted with the new Freedom of Contract rule as they can now negotiate their own transfers at the end of a contract.

My last conversation with Gordon Lee came when he told me a big London club was interested and I was to go and see Lord Westwood. 'When you get there I don't care what you say about me', he said. The last thing I wanted was trouble, all I needed was a different club and the start of a new era.

I knew what the chairman would ask me before I even got to our meeting. 'Do you want to play for Newcastle United Football Club again?' I explained to him that it was a question of professional satisfaction. 'I can't work with the manager', I said. He even brought up something I shouted at our supporters after one of Newcastle's Wembley defeats. 'You told them we would win it next time, Malcolm', he reminded me. 'Will there be a next time?' After an hour he must have known I could not go back and he just said: 'I suggest you go home immediately. Terry Neill of Arsenal will be contacting you.'

It is funny but Lord Westwood never once asked me if I wanted to play for Arsenal. It was just accepted.

The telephone was ringing as I walked through the front door. It was Terry Neill: 'I am chartering a plane and will be at Newcastle Airport in two hours. Can you be there?' he asked.

And that was it. Simple. One phone call and I was on my way to sign for Arsenal. Surely nothing would go wrong now ....

7

Welcome to Highbury

The tiny four-seater plane droned towards Luton Airport with a very contented man aboard. I was happy and excited about signing for Arsenal. I had always heard they did things in style and this was first class.

Terry Neill, the club's Irish manager, had chartered a plane to bring me down from Newcastle. If he did it to impress me he had succeeded. He wanted me as his first major signing for Arsenal and I was ready to play for one of the biggest clubs in the world.

The jovial atmosphere didn't change when Arsenal secretary Ken Friar met us at Luton or when we went to Neill's home in Potters Bar for dinner and brandies into the early hours of the next morning. There had been no hard transfer talk but it didn't matter. That would start in the morning. I slept like a baby that night.

I stayed as a guest in Terry Neill's house for three days. He and his wife Sandra were the perfect hosts ... but there was something wrong. We talked, went to Highbury, but nothing was said about a contract, money or completing the deal. The start of the 1976-77 season was only a few weeks away and I was keen to get things sorted out. Why wouldn't Arsenal talk terms?

It was an unreal situation and it hadn't changed when I was moved into the nearby West Lodge Park Hotel the following week. Julie and the children came down to London but all I could tell them was: 'Sorry, but we may have to go home again. Arsenal don't seem that interested.'

It was at this stage that I had a telephone call from Sidney Wale, the much-respected former chairman of Spurs. I did not take it as an illegal approach. My contract with Newcastle had finished and news of my delay in signing for Arsenal was in every national newspaper.

A few hours later I sat talking to Bill Nicholson, Tottenham's former manager and now a vital backroom boy. Bill asked me if I was interested in signing for Spurs and my answer had to be yes because I just didn't know if Arsenal still wanted me. Terry Neill had not made anything clear.

Looking back, that was an incredible meeting. I was a guest of Arsenal's at an expensive hotel and yet I sat in the car park talking to their great rivals.

Tottenham's interest froze the moment I mentioned that Newcastle's asking price was £275,000. 'We are just not in that kind of league', Nicholson said. My transfer talks with a First Division club in London had finished in a matter of minutes.

It took a delightful old gentleman to bring some sanity to a week in London. Terry Neill took me to the Hartley Wintney home of Denis Hill Wood, Arsenal's Old Etonian chairman. It was about 4.45 in the afternoon when we knocked at his front door. 'So you have finally arrived' were his first words. 'You have made me miss my tea, so it looks like a gin and tonic in the garden. Would you care to join us?'

I warmed to Hill Wood immediately and he came to the point straight away. 'I am having a lot of problems signing you from the Newcastle end', he went on. 'They are waiting for all their directors to agree on a price, so I have upped our offer to £300,000.'

I spent an enjoyable hour at the chairman's home, drinking and talking with his wife and son-in-law Tony Wood, another Arsenal director. We waited for a telephone call from Newcastle chairman Lord Westwood to confirm the deal. I felt relaxed and wanted. Why hadn't Terry Neill explained the problems to me before? It was the first of many mysteries I experienced at Highbury.

Lord Westwood rang to say Newcastle had accepted the offer, only to call back fifteen minutes later and ask: 'Who is going to pay the extras?' I heard Hill Wood shout: 'I will go to one third of a million. No more.' He was certainly a man of his word and told me: 'I want to sign you, Malcolm, but if they don't accept this offer the deal is off. I'm sorry.'

I spent an anxious ten minutes waiting for Westwood to phone again and confirm the transfer. It was a fascinating insight for me into how transfer deals are sometimes done. One more bungling phone call from Newcastle and I wouldn't have signed for Arsenal.

The fee was finally settled at £333,333, 33p, Arsenal's record signing. The next day I met Terry Neill at Highbury to discuss the details of my contract.

I was in a good position. Arsenal had come for me, I had the best goalscoring record in the First Division and was in the England squad. I invited my accountant, Howard Withers, along to advise me and witness what I thought was going to be a straightforward deal. I didn't know at the time but that Saturday morning meeting was the start of a frustrating and bitter relationship I had with Terry Neill. It was not long before I lost all respect for the man.

I will explain in detail what happened at and after that business meeting between the three of us.

My salary at Newcastle had been £300 a week basic plus £2,000 a year if I played 35 competitive matches and another £2,000 if I scored 25 first team goals. I was obviously not going to sign for less and yet I laughed aloud when Terry Neill told me Arsenal's basic wage and loyalty bonus scheme. It would have meant a drop in salary.

I told him I wanted £380 a week basic plus a full share of the bonus and loyalty and the contract to be re-negotiable every year. After much haggling Terry Neill wrote all this down and the three of us shook hands. It was a gentleman's agreement.

Arsenal were going on tour to Yugoslavia the following week and Terry wanted me in the squad. I was ready now to sign a contract but he explained there was no independent witness or office staff in on Saturday to draw one up.

Neill however then asked me if I would sign a blank contract and the details would be filled in while the team were away.

My accountant, who was with us the entire time, agreed. A gentleman's agreement was binding. I repeated that I would only sign for Arsenal for the figures and clauses we had shaken hands on.

A sick feeling spread up from my stomach the moment I opened my first wage slip. I couldn't believe what I saw. I rushed into see Arsenal's wages clerk and said: 'I should get more than that a week'. His reply was stunning. 'A week? That is two weeks' wages. Arsenal players get paid twice a month.'

I walked straight into secretary Ken Friar's office and demanded to see my contract. There it was in black and white, £156 a week, a basic wage of less than half what I had negotiated, and with my signature on the bottom.

I told the entire story to Ken Friar and he was staggered at the amount of money I had agreed with Terry Neill. He said that no-one there was on that kind of money. This was the first deal that he had not been involved with at the contract negotiating stage. If he had been in on our talks I would not have signed for Arsenal.

If that had happened I would have gone abroad to play. I would not have signed for anyone for the figures staring up at me from my contract.

I was bitterly angry and Ken Friar probably caught the wrong end of my temper. My ultimatum was simple: if you don't get anything sorted out, I don't play. I was set to lose £10,000 per year. I agreed to go back and see him in a month after he had discussed it at boardroom level.

It was impossible to enjoy one day of my first four weeks at Arsenal. There was a cloud hanging over me. I felt cheated. I made my debut on the first day of the season against Bristol City and was introduced to the crowd before the kick-off.

I looked at the faces from the centre spot where I stood waving. They were laughing, cheering me. I was their new hero and they expected so much. I wanted to run over to each one of them and tell them what was going on behind the scenes. Did they agree with me, was I doing the right thing? There was a possibility that in a month I would not be an Arsenal player. I would have walked out if the board had not supported me.

During that month Terry Neill did not explain anything. I can't believe he wasn't consulted and yet the only words we had came as we passed each other one day in the Highbury corridors. 'I understand there has been a little misunderstanding over your contract', he said. I ignored him and from that day I felt only contempt towards him.

In the dressing room before a game he would say to us: 'Come on, lads, battle for me, do it for me today'. Do it for him! I was on the verge of taking Arsenal to court. I didn't feel like playing, let alone battling for someone I wasn't sure about.

To my great relief Ken Friar and the board sorted everything out. When I went back into his office a month later there was a new four-year contract drawn up for the start of the following 1977-78 season which included a special clause inserted for a payment of £10,500. It was a good feeling to know the board had backed me.

It wasn't long before we fell out again and once more it was

over a term in our gentleman's agreement. My new terms for the
1978-79 season had not been re-negotiated. I spoke to Terry
Neill about it. He said he was unaware of my right to re-negotiate the financial terms annually, but he would check his notes
of our first meeting and put it to the board. Five weeks later, the
day before the season opened with a home game against Leeds,
Terry told me: 'I have been meaning to see you. There is nothing
we can do.'

I returned once more to Ken Friar and his reaction was that he
had thought everything had been sorted out, but that he would
look into it immediately. So I had still not signed a new contract
and they had to be with the Football League the next morning,
the day of the new season.

Overnight Arsenal gave me a cost-of-living allowance of £40,
taking my basic salary to £420 a week. Ken had prevented
another situation occurring and once again the board had been
understanding. I signed on the morning of the match and
Arsenal got special clearance for me to play against Leeds.

It wouldn't surprise me if Terry Neill banned me from
Highbury for repeating these stories. If that happened I would
be punished for telling the truth. I have often been criticized for
being too controversial and yet it is only honesty. This is what
happened.

It would have been easy to gloss over the details but they are
very important to me. I would also love to hear Terry Neill's side
of what happened between our handshake and the day I opened
my first wage slip.

8

The mystery of Arsenal

When Bill Shankly pinned up a sign announcing 'This is Anfield' at the end of the players' tunnel, even he couldn't have realized how much apprehension those three words would strike into Liverpool's opponents. It was a master stroke by a man who wanted his Liverpool to be feared by the rest of football. The sign stares down as you step out in front of the Kop, and the psychological effect is the same even when you make your tenth visit.

At Highbury there is no such sign, only the smell of history to greet you. It is rather like walking into a museum as a commissionaire welcomes you into marbled halls and a staircase dominated by a black, highly polished bust of Herbert Chapman. You don't need a printed guide to read that Arsenal are a great football club.

And the effect is the same as Shankly's sign. Players are either lifted or destroyed by the atmosphere.

Highbury is a stadium for the VIP. It has a reputation throughout football of being the best and that is exactly how it is. Arsenal treat their players like members of an exclusive club and of course the word spreads throughout football. When Arsenal are in town there is either envy or jealousy from opposing players and supporters.

Arsenal's name is so big and their reputation so good that they receive more invitations to play abroad than any other club in the country. It is very rare for a player to turn down the chance of playing for Arsenal and when he signs and settles in he doesn't usually want to leave. There are not many men who have chosen to quit Arsenal — Ray Kennedy of Liverpool is an exception — and gone on to become a better and more successful player.

George Armstrong, who spent almost his entire career as an Arsenal player and became one of Highbury's all-time favourites, soon discovered life can be very different when he joined Leicester. 'I just didn't appreciate how much Arsenal do for their players', Armstrong told me. 'For years I have taken all the little things for granted. I thought it was the same throughout football. I am glad I experienced the other side of the water before I retired.'

All an Arsenal player basically has to do is train and play. The rest of his life is taken care for him. He is like a millionaire staying at the best hotel. If he doesn't like the laces in his boots Arsenal will change them, if he wants a certain soup before his meal on the club's luxury coach Arsenal will get it, and then there is secretary Ken Friar waiting in the background to solve any personal or financial problems the players may have.

I have always maintained that if ever I became manager of a football club I would try and persuade Friar to join me. He is the best, an administrator who could walk into any top business in this country and do a good job.

The other person I would offer a job to is Tony Donnelly, the man who 'looks after' the players in the dressing room. Tony knows everything about every Arsenal first team player and their problems are his, however small. He knew that I liked to wear baggy shorts and it was his responsibility to make sure they were always hanging on my peg. He checks boots for splits and missing studs, even replacing laces if there is a chance one might break during a game.

At Newcastle I always had to look after my own boots and training footwear. That is unheard-of at Arsenal; even at the training headquarters at London Colney your boots and kit are laid out waiting for you every day, cleaned and ironed. Arsenal's attitude is if a player has to worry about anything except training and playing it could affect his performance.

And yet, despite Arsenal's reputation of respect and grandeur throughout the world, there remains a certain mystery surrounding the club. It is the Buckingham Palace of football. No-one knows exactly what is going on behind the closed doors.

The players are the employees and, despite being treated magnificently, there is an upstairs-downstairs relationship.

When I was at Newcastle the club was an open book, there were no secrets, no pages missing and the public were allowed inside to share the glory and the disappointments. If a Working Man's Club wanted Bobby Moncur to go as guest speaker, the club made sure he went. We were all a very close family, the board, the players and the supporters.

That can never be said of Arsenal and that is why Terry Neill is an ideal manager for them. He retains that mystery, never allowing you into his mind or selling you the warmth that supporters should feel towards their football club.

Terry is what is known as a front-man; he is not a good team manager but an ideal public relations figure. He is brilliant at talking for hours and not telling you a thing. His Irish tones wash over you like a long-playing record, and your initial reaction is: 'What a great bloke'. Then you analyse your conversation and he hasn't given you any straight answers or taken you into his confidence.

It can be extremely frustrating for players, especially when it happens a number of times. They start turning to other people for answers — the secretary, the coach and, in Arsenal's case, even the chairman.

There is no doubt in my mind that the best and perhaps luckiest thing that happened to Terry Neill at Highbury was the arrival of Don Howe. It was the greatest investment the club have made, for Howe certainly stopped a players' revolution.

We didn't respect the manager's coaching, which is the worst thing that can happen to anyone in authority. Before Don Howe arrived it was Terry and his No. 2 Wilf Dixon in charge, and the training sessions were almost as bad as the debacle I experienced under Gordon Lee and Richard Dinnis at Newcastle. We were not playing for Terry Neill, we were playing for Arsenal and, to be fair to Terry, he probably realized it. At least he was big enough to urge Arsenal to go out and get the best. Don Howe is the best.

Howe immediately communicated with the players, understood our problems. It was Howe we wanted to take all the coaching, Howe we turned to when things went wrong on the pitch.

There was always an amusing incident every Saturday before a home game. Arsenal take their players to the South Herts Golf Club, Totteridge, for a final build-up and after a light lunch, television or a game of snooker the players move into the committee room for a last team talk. Terry always says the same thing: 'It is going to be hard to-day, you have to fight for me, battle for the club', and then turns to Don Howe and asks: 'Have you got anything to add, Don?' For the next 30 minutes Howe builds his team up and details any problems we might have to cancel out.

Terry Neill does let his public image slip occasionally and after one heavy home defeat he described us as 'morons' to the millions of *Match of the Day* viewers. I watched the programme with Julie and she just exploded, wanting to ring Terry and complain. We ended up having a terrible row over something he had said.

The definition of 'moron' is 'a mentally deficient person' and I almost took legal action over the remark. My solicitor advised me that I could get a public apology and £5,000 damages. If all the other players had taken similar action, it would have cost Terry Neill around £60,000. So much for a good PRO.

Alan Hudson relates a story that questions Neill's relationship with players. A Spanish club wanted to sign Alan, and Terry, Huddy and the club's representative met at Highbury. After initial talks Terry was asked how much Arsenal wanted for Hudson. When he was told the fee would be £150,000, the man said: 'That is good because we have allocated £250,000 for this transfer. We pay Arsenal £150,000 and the player gets £100,000 signing-on fee.'

With that Terry Neill is alleged to have ended the conversation and called the deal off. It was a desperate blow to Hudson because he wanted to get away from Arsenal and the money, of course, would have set him up. 'It would have been a great move for me', Hudson told me later. 'Terry just wasn't interested. He and I didn't get on but I can't believe he would have stopped it because of that.'

The relationship between Arsenal players also seems to be affected by the polished atmosphere at Highbury. While we worked well together there were no regular social evenings for the team and their wives to enjoy. At Newcastle, Frank Clark, John Tudor and I used to spend hours at a local milk bar talking and putting the world right. We were all good friends but I never struck up that kind of relationship at Arsenal. There was no animosity between the team members and I got on well with people like Alan Ball, Alan Hudson, David O'Leary and Frank Stapleton, but we never got close enough to call each other good friends.

Liam Brady, so magnificently expressive and dominating on the pitch, is another Arsenal player it is hard to communicate with. Alan Ball was a big influence on Brady's early career and the two of them had a telepathic understanding during the game. Off it they were two opposites. That is typical of football.

Two men can hate each other in private life, but if they respect each other's ability, football draws them together. There was no reason why John Tudor and I should get on so well, but we were both strikers playing alongside each other every week and grew together. A relationship was born from discussing the same problems and facing the same pressures on the pitch.

After Ball's departure Brady then influenced, sometimes dominated, his next midfield partner Graham Rix. At the start they were not especially the best of friends, but football threw them together. Brady and Rix, the names go together like Clough and Taylor. They are working at the same things, they understand each other. Brady helped Rix blossom into an even better player.

I look back on my three years at Arsenal with pleasure. I had spells of aggravation but it doesn't hide the fact that I played for one of the biggest club sides in the world. I'm sorry Arsenal didn't see the very best of Malcolm Macdonald and that injury cut short my career, but 42 First Division goals in 84 matches is not a bad record.

Arsenal are more than a football club. They are an institution and, while the tradition of Highbury never allowed me to feel completely at home, I am proud to say that I played for the best club in English football.

That no doubt will throw up screams of dispute from Manchester United and Liverpool but Old Trafford and Anfield have not the aura of Highbury.

9

Sent home in disgrace

There is not a man on this earth who would not react to being labelled a trouble-maker and a rebel. I have always spoken out against things I don't believe are right and that has often led to controversy, but I have never deliberately tried to cause aggravation. Yet I was branded a rebel on 24 July 1977 when I flew into a crowded Heathrow Airport. Arsenal had sent me home in disgrace, suspended and transfer-listed, from their pre-season tour of Singapore and Australia.

The reason was an alleged drinking incident but of course the cause of my early arrival back in London goes far deeper. The punishment of being sent home and the abuse I received afterwards remain the only major blemish on my character in ten years of football. It is a black mark I bitterly dispute.

I was even accused of being drunk on arrival at Heathrow Airport and criticized for not talking to waiting pressmen. I still would have remained silent today if Arsenal manager Terry Neill had not discussed me when he returned with the rest of the squad 24 hours later. This is the first time I have told the entire story of what happened 'Down Under'; it doesn't wipe away the memory completely but it helps. It also explains the demands on players when a famous club like Arsenal travel abroad.

I was sent home with Alan Hudson. No doubt half of the football-minded people in this country will have found us guilty without knowing what really happened. Poor Alan was unjustly tarred with the same brush 24 hours a day. One of the great players England has produced has seen his career ruined by managers who can't and don't want to understand him and by people who don't even know him.

Every time I bring Alan's name up in conversation the reaction is usually the same: 'Oh him, Hudson's just a trouble-maker'. This is from people who have never met him! It is one of the great pressures footballers have to live with, as members of the public identify themselves and pass judgement on the stars they see on television or read about in newspapers.

Hudson admits that he is not entirely blameless for a wasted career. He has done things, said things, that he regrets but has never found a manager to carry him through little personal crises. Tony Waddington at Stoke briefly treated Huddy properly but at Chelsea, Arsenal and with England under Don Revie he was allowed to disappear.

In Singapore and Australia we were basically punished for speaking out against things that were obviously wrong. There was a lot of aggravation for the players and since I have never been one to sit back and say nothing, I'm sure I said what all the other players thought.

My own problems began before Arsenal were due to leave, when I was invited to play in Australia for the South Melbourne side Hellas. They wanted me for a month and offered my family and me a villa on Shark Island as accommodation. It was a wonderful opportunity for us and I arranged with Hellas that I would meet up with Arsenal the moment they touched down at the start of their tour.

Arsenal were not keen. Terry Neill said I would miss three days' training before the rest of the party flew out. I waited for a final decision and was eventually told I could go for ten days. 'Ten days?' I said. 'It takes four to get there and back.' I finally got it extended to sixteen and I left, without my family, played for Hellas and travelled all the way back again. Then I turned around and flew to Singapore with Arsenal. It was a crazy decision. Instead of meeting up with Arsenal in peak condition I was in the wrong frame of mind and suffering from jet lag.

All pre-season tours are negotiated outside the players' contracts. The country or organizing body who invite the club guarantee a certain fee and the players are paid a further sum. We were promised by Terry Neill an eventual total well in excess of £1,000 each for that tour although in the end the players received less than half. Because I was sent home I didn't collect a penny and the whole shambles cost me £300 out of my own pocket.

When we asked about money to spend during the trip, the answer was always 'tomorrow', which built up tremendous ill-feeling amongst the players.

In Singapore, Arsenal played in a four-cornered competition against Red Star Belgrade, Celtic and the home national team.

The temperature was often in the 90s and the humidity so high that we sweated and lost an awful lot of weight during a game. Doctor Sach's advice afterwards was always the same: 'Drink only water or beer to allow your body to return to normal'.

The pressure on the players mounted as we spent our own money and were then asked to act as smiling ambassadors for the club.

We were once ushered to a local store as a publicity stunt to sign autographs and have our photographs taken. No footballer minds doing these kind of things but we were reluctant to co-operate because of Arsenal's attitude towards the financial side of the trip. Our attitude was: 'Someone is getting paid for a stunt like this, but we haven't seen a penny since we left London'. Had we been given out spending money and the promises been supported, we would have thrown ourselves into promoting Arsenal during the tour.

Alan Hudson, George Armstrong and I decided we had suffered enough and walked out of the store. It only needed us to make a decision and the rest of the players followed. Yet because we were the first through the door we were named as the ring-leaders, the players who had given the club a bad name.

Tiny incidents began to snowball to disillusion the players. Although we were told to drink a lot of liquid by the club doctor, our refrigerator in the rooms only contained one large bottle of orange and two Cokes for the entire eight days we spent in Singapore. On paper these things probably appear petty and incidental, but they helped build up unnecessary pressure.

Our reputation with the manager didn't improve after another incident while we watched Celtic take on Singapore. An Englishman sitting behind the Arsenal players began pestering me with stupid comments and loud accusations. He was one of a number of bores at the ground who didn't know Arsenal from Newport County or who any of the players were. We decided to watch the match from a bar at the back of the stand that over-looked the ground and met six Scottish lads, real football supporters, who were thrilled at watching their favourite club, Celtic, again. We told a ground official to explain to Terry Neill where we were, but Arsenal didn't wait and the coach left without us. The official party still only beat us back to the hotel restaurant by three minutes but it didn't save our first row with Neill. He demanded to know where we had been and we told him Arsenal should treat their players like human beings. 'You move us around like a pack of penguins', I said. 'We are men, not robots.'

I may have been an Arsenal player but no-one owns my pride. We were being treated like schoolboys and I was just not prepared to accept it.

We told Terry there was a bad feeling running through the players and he obviously blamed us. The split between the manager and the three of us widened when exactly the same incident occurred when we returned to the same ground to watch Celtic play Red Star. Yet there was no fuss on our part and we certainly didn't make a scene or fools of ourselves in public.

The next morning Terry decided to get his own back during training. 'Right, you had your fun, I'm going to slaughter you now', he said. But all he succeeded in doing was to punish the other players. George Armstrong and Hudson can run all day and I was determined not to be beaten.

Willie Young, Arsenal's big Scottish defender, began to struggle and Neill tore into him. 'You are out of order', I shouted. 'You are saying to him what you should be saying to me.'

That riled him even more and he took us on to the track for sprint-lapping against the clock. Talk about mad dogs and Englishmen. The temperature was up in the 90s and there we were racing around. The other players began to moan and blame us for the punishment. Armstrong and Hudson found their six half-laps easy and then angered Neill even more by applauding me all the way around as I strained to make it. I even did an extra lap to prove to Neill that he hadn't got the better of me. His answer was to take us into the gym for yet another work-out.

Again all this sounds stupid now but at the time it was a test of character between the manager and the three of us. We were unhappy with each other and both sides refused to break. And still there was no spending money.

Our arrival in Australia didn't change anything. The beds were so small my feet stuck out at the end and it was impossible to get a good night's sleep. When I complained about the rooms to one of the tour organizers, Tommy Lawrence, he said: 'You are nothing but a trouble-maker, moaning all the time. You complain about anything.' So the word had spread throughout the party; I was the bad boy.

Terry Neill's answer was the same when I complained about

the rooms. 'Manchester United stay here and I have been here before with Tottenham', he said. 'So why isn't it good enough for you?'

Compared with our hotel in Singapore, our first accommodation in Australia was second-class. It was a one-night hotel and an uncomfortable one at that! 'Why should I have to put up with sleeping in a cot?' I demanded. With that Terry Neill just walked away.

My composure just broke. Aggravation, no money and now this. I didn't see any point in staying with Arsenal and went to collect my air tickets and passport from secretary Ken Friar, who was staying with the officials in a magnificent hotel a few miles away. 'I'm going home, Ken, and I don't care if I never play for Arsenal again. Everything has gone wrong once more', I told him.

Friar was staggered when I told him how much we had been promised for the tour. 'It's impossible', he said. 'You just couldn't have been offered that kind of money.' It was the same old story, a promise that had absolutely no chance of being kept.

For the second time since I arrived at Highbury Ken persuaded me from walking out on Arsenal. It didn't clear the atmosphere, however, and things went from bad to worse as we lost to Celtic 3-2 and were slaughtered 3-1 by Australia.

Alan Hudson and I may not have been angels on the tour but no-one could fault our playing performances. Huddy was Man of the Match against Red Star and brilliant against Singapore and Celtic, and I got five goals in four games including a hat-trick against Singapore. We were still prepared to battle despite the bad feeling and outside pressures.

Terry Neill and the club knew I wanted to go home when we travelled from Sydney to Adelaide. It was a tiring journey and we didn't arrive until lunch time, only 24 hours before a game against Red Star. Huddy and I were shattered after our sleepless nights in the previous hotel and we decided to have a meal, take a Mogadon sleeping pill with a gin and tonic and go straight to bed.

In the bar, Dennis Hill Wood and Tony Wood offered to buy us a drink and, although we refused, the chairman insisted (in his defence, he may not have known that we were drinking gin and tonics). Halfway through our lunch of rare steaks and salad Terry Neill came over, pointed at our glasses and said: 'Is that what I think it is?' and stormed off.

On our way upstairs to sleep, skipper Pat Rice broke the news that we were training that afternoon. 'Don't be crazy, Pat', we said. 'We can't train, we have just taken a sleeping pill. All we want to do is go to bed.'

Alan and I were both fast asleep when Terry came crashing into our bedroom and ordered us to get up. 'Right, you two, we are training, get ready.' We couldn't even speak properly, let alone start running around.

'Don't be silly, Terry, you didn't tell us we were training, you are out of order to spring it on us like this', I slurred into my pillow.

He then told us we were both being sent home. 'That's good', I answered, 'I wanted to go a week ago.' And that was the now-famous drinks incident — two gin and tonics, one innocently bought by chairman Denis Hill Wood — and our last conversation with Neill for a long time.

Ken Friar escorted us to the airport and it took us 33 hours to get home as we travelled via Adelaide, Melbourne, Sydney, Bahrain and Rome to return to Heathrow. It was the longest way home possible and the ridiculous thing was that Arsenal arrived back at Heathrow the following day. A lot of fuss and controversy could have been avoided if we had returned together and then Arsenal had punished us quietly a few days later.

The return flight and the disgrace of being sent home turned into a special occasion for us when we met three lovely old ladies returning to England after a holiday of a lifetime around-the-world. We were supposed to be in disgrace but their happiness made us forget our problems. It was the biggest occasion of their lives and 30 minutes out of Heathrow we ordered champagne and turned on some music.

'Well, ladies', I said. 'You are travelling with two naughty boys sent home from the wilderness. How about dancing your way back home?'

It was a party atmosphere from then on and by the time we touched down everyone on board was singing and waltzing in the aisle. It was a happy ending to a very unhappy tour.

We had contacted our wives from Australia to meet us at Heathrow, but we knew there would be a reception committee waiting for us. First, we decided not to say anything to anyone and just sang 'All pals together' as we hurried through the crowd and back to Alan's house to discuss the entire situation.

We were both suspended for two weeks and transfer-listed,

and although I eventually repaired my split with Arsenal, the gap between Alan and Terry Neill was too wide. He stuck it out for another season and even played against Ipswich in the FA Cup Final the following May, but it was inevitable that he would eventually leave Highbury. The club became the onlooker in a two-way fight between the manager and a player. There was a brick wall between them.

The only reason I came off the transfer list was Arsenal's father figure, chairman Denis Hill Wood. Just as I had before when I signed for the club, I visited Hill Wood's Hampshire home to discuss the future. I got the impression he didn't want me to leave and after talks that lasted all afternoon I was happy to stay.

It is strange that all through my career at Arsenal I never looked on Terry Neill as my boss. He was the manager of the club but I just couldn't accept him as a man to look up to. Perhaps it is my fault, but he didn't inspire respect or confidence in me. I was playing for Arsenal, for the chairman if you like.

I expect that the conclusion of many people to our saga 'Down Under' will be that the Arsenal players were being greedy and that Hudson and I behaved badly. I can honestly say I would react in exactly the same way if the same problems occurred.

Arsenal are one of the biggest club sides in the world and there is no reason why their employees should have promises broken, be kept waiting for spending money, be treated like school-children or be unhappy with living accommodation. We are grown men, professional people at the top. We are not fools, and it was obvious that someone got paid an awful lot of money for Arsenal to travel and play in Singapore and Australia. These tours are money-making ventures for big clubs like Arsenal. On this occasion it certainly wasn't for the players.

Alan Hudson and I got into trouble because we dared to question the system, although George Armstrong asked to be sent home with us but Terry Neill refused. I am not proud of being sent home. We were only guilty of being rebels and trouble-makers if it is a crime to fight for what is yours. Anyone with character would have done the same.

10

My worst hat-trick

Wembley Stadium at 4.40 in the afternoon on Cup Final Saturday is no place for a loser. I should know, I have suffered the humiliation and dreadful anti-climax of defeat three times.

It is the only hat-trick of my career I want to forget. Newcastle were murdered 3-0 by Liverpool in the 1974 FA Cup Final, two years later Manchester City beat us 2-1 in the League Cup, and then in 1978 came perhaps the most bitter pill of all to swallow. Arsenal were beaten by the underdogs from Ipswich in the FA Cup Final.

When the referee blows his final whistle to split Wembley down the middle into happiness and horror there is nothing anyone can do for you. At the end of Arsenal's defeat by Ipswich I can remember looking up to the sky and thinking, 'Not a third time! Why me?'

The capacity crowd of 100,000 looks down and every loser thinks all eyes are trained on him. There are hundreds of people chasing around on the pitch but suddenly you feel lonely. You don't want to say anything. The last thing you want to do is go and collect your loser's medal.

Wembley becomes a ritual of events you know you must accept with as much grace as your bitterness will allow. Shake hands with the VIPs in the Royal Box, wave to the supporters, jog back to the dressing room, go back to the hotel, get changed and put on a brave face at the banquet.

The pressures that go with an FA Cup Final are tremendous. When a player reports for pre-season training in July his thoughts are on one thing: To win something. The League Championship is accepted as the outstanding team performance, the Cup Final is the icing on the cake. Players lie awake at night dreaming of playing in the final. The glamour, the television coverage, the build-up; it is a wonderful experience.

Some teams treat getting to Wembley with a magnificent professional attitude. They win the game first and enjoy themselves
for the rest of the year. Others use the period from victory in the
semi-final to the great day as an excuse for a party. They are
heroes before the event, mugs afterwards.

Newcastle, I'm afraid, got out the champagne too quickly.
We didn't abuse the rules of build-up, just changed them
slightly. And on Saturday, 4 May 1974 we didn't have a chance
against Bill Shankly's superbly prepared Liverpool.

It is amazing how we even found our way to Wembley. Our
path through the rounds was littered with scares, controversy
and amazing incidents. We started with a 1-1 home draw
against non-League Hendon and after winning the replay 4-0 at
Watford slumped even lower by drawing at home to Scunthorpe
in the fourth round.

We were so bad we hardly crossed the halfway line and it was
completely unexpected when Terry McDermott kept us in the
Cup with a magnificent goal from 35 yards. We won the replay
3-0 and then produced our best performance of the season in
beating West Brom 3-0 at the Hawthorns. In front of 10,000
Geordies who had travelled to the Midlands we played football
that any team in the country would have been proud of. It was
typical of the Newcastle side I played in. One day we were
magnificent, the next pathetic.

The sixth round draw gave us another home tie, this time
against Second Division Nottingham Forest and surely we
couldn't frustrate our fans again. We not only sent them crazy
with frustration, we ran headlong into one of the most controversial incidents in the history of the FA Cup.

Forest took the lead through Ian Bowyer, before David Craig
made it 1-1, but Liam O'Kane and then a George Lyall penalty
seemingly put Forest into the semi-final. Pat Howard protested
so strongly over the penalty that he was sent off, and that was too
much for our supporters. Having watched us struggle against
Hendon, and Scunthorpe in earlier rounds, they poured on to St
James' Park in their hundreds. I don't believe there was aggro in
their minds, only that they couldn't hide their emotions any
longer. Referee Gordon Kew had no alternative but to take all
the players back into the dressing room while the police cleared
the pitch. When we returned Forest were obviously shaken by
the incident and had no stomach for the rest of the match. Terry
McDermott made it 3-2 from a penalty, John Tudor equalized

and then, with the last kick of the game, and under more noise than I can ever remember hearing from a football crowd, Bobby Moncur made it 4-3.

Forest, however, protested that their players had been attacked by our supporters and, while Newcastle officials argued that Nottingham had accepted the decision to continue, the Football Association wiped out the match and ordered it to be replayed at Everton's Goodison Park home.

After the emotions of every player had been stretched to the limit by the incredible happenings at St James' Park it is not surprising that the replay ended in a goalless draw. I thought I had won the game for Newcastle when, through on my own, I lobbed the ball over Jim Barron only to see it hit a divot and bounce wide.

Forest then received a kick in the teeth when the FA ordered a second replay to take place at Goodison Park again three days later. Forest argued they had done enough to take the tie to their own ground, and deep down we all agreed with them.

It was another lucky break for us in our Cup run and this time I did score to put Newcastle into the semi-final with Burnley. It meant that I had scored in every round and I promised the local press boys that I would get us to Wembley. I was called the Muhammed Ali of football for making the predictions, but I honestly felt confident of scoring against Burnley. I didn't think anything could stop us now. After what had happened to us since the third round on 5 January this must be our year.

I kept to my promise and Terry McDermott and Terry Hibbitt sent me through for our two goals. Colin Waldron did his best to stop the first, climbing all over my back as I raced into the area. He fell off as I shot and when the ball rebounded from Alan Stevenson I scored. It was a superb advantage rule decision by referee Gordon Hill and afterwards he admitted to me: 'I don't know what I would have done if you had missed. It was so obviously a foul and I just sweated on you scoring.'

Having played nine matches to get to Wembley, surely we had done the hard work. If we could just turn it on when it mattered. ... The coach journey back from Hillsborough to Newcastle was like a party and the words of Reg Hayter, who was elected to run our players' pool for the final, were alas forgotten. He told us: 'You are Cup finalists for one day, Cup holders for a year'.

It is advice every player getting to Wembley should appreciate. It is no good being in the Miss World contest if you don't end up with the crown on your head. If you lose you might as well go home to Mum. It is the same at Wembley, losers are forgotten before *Grandstand* is over.

The atmosphere in the North East during the weeks building up to Wembley were fantastic. Everyone wanted to know us, it was as if we had won the Cup already. Wembley is the Mecca for Geordie supporters, They would rather win the Final than the League.

You don't appreciate what you are doing wrong until after the event. We did crazy things like cut training short by 30 minutes to get to a recording studio to make our Wembley record. Coach Keith Burkinshaw didn't like what was going on but Joe Harvey would say: 'They will be OK', and we didn't need any excuse to forget about football.

Even in the final week incidents piled on top of each other. My Jensen Healey car lost its gear box en route to St James' Park on the Monday morning and I missed the first day's training of our Wembley build-up.

Then on the Wednesday I had to go to the *Daily Mirror* offices in London for a picture special for their Wembley pull-out paper on the day of the match. While I waited afterwards for an ordered car to take me back to our Selsdon Park, Croydon head-quarters, I had a couple of drinks with the girl reporter doing the article in a pub called The White Hart, affectionately known to *Mirror* men as 'The Stab'. We were just leaving by the front entrance when the girl pushed me back into the pub and dragged me out of the back door. 'What the hell's going on?' I screamed at her. Apparently there had been a photographer waiting outside to take a picture of Malcolm Macdonald leaving a pub only three days before Wembley.

With only 24 hours to go before Newcastle's record eleventh Wembley final we still had not received our black and white tracksuits. The man from Burtons eventually turned up on Friday afternoon with an all-white, black trim towelling suit. They had webbed arms and legs and we were all adamant: 'We are not wearing those'. Terry Hibbitt tried one on to prove how stupid we would look and he was right; Terry pranced around the hotel looking just like a penguin.

A frantic phone call to Gola got us out of trouble, but they didn't have a set of black and white suits. They could only find twelve purple and yellow ones and that is why Newcastle, the famous Magpies, walked out at Wembley in purple!

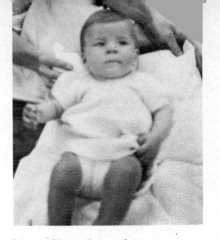

Mum, I'm going to be a star.
Me aged ten months.

Brother James (*right*) and I
with our father.

Me aged twelve in my
Sloane Grammar School
uniform.

The goal that upset Johnny Haynes. I score against Blackburn with the great man in the background and Frank Large on the right.

Opposite:
Welcome to Newcastle. I proudly try the famous black and white shirt on for size on my first day at St James' Park.

Alan Slough and I celebrate another goal and happy days at Luton. Shrewsbury centre half Alf Wood doesn't look too pleased, though.

Terry Neill, then player-manager of Hull City, and I clash for the first time during a Second Division match in 1970.

Helped off by Keith Burkinshaw and Newcastle physiotherapist
Alec Mutch, after scoring a hat-trick on my home debut.

The misery of Wembley. Another defeat for Newcastle after
Manchester City had beaten us in the League Cup Final.

Two Newcastle idols together. I interview the great Jackie Milburn on my programme for Radio Newcastle.

I head in England's second goal, during the England versus West Germany football international at Wembley Stadium.

Don Revie and I during England training.

Happiness is scoring. Arsenal captain Alan Ball congratulates me
after one of my hat-trick goals against Newcastle.

My wife Julie meets me at Heathrow Airport after I was sent home
by Arsenal from Australia.

My last Wembley journey. I walk alone back to the dressing room after Ipswich had beaten Arsenal in the 1978 FA Cup Final.

With my two great friends Harry Haslam (*left*) and Joe Harvey.

I could sense we were not completely ready but the game was fast approaching. Television cameras on the coach didn't help, the lights, cables and silly questions made it a harrowing journey down Wembley Way.

While we were getting changed, the words of wise old Alec Stock echoed in my head. He had told his Queen's Park Rangers players before their League Cup Final against West Brom: 'If I see any of you waving to your family or celebrating before the game there will be trouble. We are here to win and I want you only to wave with a winner's medal in your hand.' My team-mates seemed too full of themselves, we were over-confident.

Suddenly the game was on top of us. We were ready to walk out, but were we mentally right? Liverpool looked so composed and immaculate in their blazing red track suits with their names printed in large letters on the back. I felt embarrassed that we were in purple.

As we stood to attention for the national anthem and the introduction to the VIPs, I looked down the line at our team and wondered what they were thinking. It was a good side — Iam McFaul, Frank Clark, Pat Howard, Bobby Moncur, Alan Kennedy, Jim Smith, Terry McDermott, Tommy Cassidy, Terry Hibbitt, John Tudor and me — and one that was capable of producing magnificent football. Would this be the day?

I was worried about a late change in our style. On Thursday Joe Harvey had decided to switch from our normal 4-3-3 formation to 4-1-2 which meant four men in midfield to combat Liverpool's strength. But Keith Burkinshaw had been given only two days to get it right.

The result was that John Tudor and I didn't get a decent pass all afternoon. We badly missed a wide man. Suddenly we had to play with our backs to goal instead of being able to push it wide and sprinting through. I still don't know how the half-time score was 0-0 and, as Frank Clark and I trooped off through the band, I said: 'We are terrible, Frank, we deserve to be beaten'.

The Newcastle heads went down when Liverpool full back Alec Lindsey had a rocket cross-shot disallowed for offside. From then on we offered only token resistance and Kevin Keegan's two goals and a third from Steve Heighway made it a miserable experience.

Bill Shankly tried hard to lift us, ignoring his players to move amongst us and offering words of help. It didn't make the dressing room a nicer place to be in and we just sat there staring into space, not daring to talk. It was Liverpool skipper Emlyn Hughes who broke the silence when he brought in the Cup, filled to the brim with champagne, and told us to drown our sorrows.

I refused because I always maintained that I would only hold the FA Cup after we had won it. I kept my promise until after I had watched Arsenal beat Manchester United in 1979. I had not played in any of Arsenal's matches but deep down I knew that I would never be returning to Wembley again.

There are a number of people who accept invitations to both Cup Final banquets and then go to the winners' party. I can remember Sir Matt Busby being the only non-Newcastle man at ours and he couldn't have enjoyed himself. No-one really cared who was there. We couldn't find the enthusiasm even to talk to each other and I just sat down with Julie, drinking and brooding. It was not the fact that we had lost to Liverpool that was so upsetting, but the way we had played. We had let down the army of Geordie supporters who had travelled to London for the greatest day in their lives.

An unlikely incident broke my tension. A girl in my party fell asleep, either out of boredom or too much to drink. A friend and I were helping her into the lift when a stranger came up and said: 'What can I do? I'm a doctor.' In the girl's bedroom he said: 'OK, you can leave her alone with me now, I'll deal with it'. I looked at him and for some reason knew that he was no more a doctor than I was a Wembley winner. I threw him out and hit him hard. With that one punch I released all the tension and frustration I had bottled up since the end of the game. At least I had hit the right man.

Two hours later I was saying goodbye to some friends when the same stranger came down the hotel steps and said: 'No hard feelings, I had to try'. I hit him again just as all the North East national press boys came out into the street. Fortunately they understood and agreed to keep 'Malcolm Macdonald's fight on Cup Final night' out of the papers.

A loser's hangover takes a long time to shake off. The depression the morning after is just as bad, as Sunday newspapers remind you of your ghastly experience.

On the train journey home to Newcastle, skipper Bobby Moncur opened a window and threw his loser's medal out and down into the River Tyne. It was how we all felt. I lost my medal years ago. It simply didn't mean anything to me.

We didn't deserve the reception the Newcastle fans gave us

when we returned home. There were thousands of Geordies, waving and singing and celebrating as if we had won. What can you say to fans who have travelled back overnight just to welcome a bunch of losers? I just screamed at them: 'We will win it for you next time'.

I meant what I said and the fact that I never helped win a Cup for Newcastle's magnificent supporters is one of the biggest regrets of my career.

At the time I didn't dream either that I would never experience the excitement of winning at Wembley in a Cup Final.

11

Another Wembley nightmare

There was only one thing on my mind when I stepped out into the bowl of light and noise that is Wembley Stadium. My left knee ached and deep down I knew I should not have been playing. I even prayed as the teams got the signal to leave the tunnel. 'Please, God, let my knee be all right this time. Just one more game.'

The pressure on Arsenal to beat Ipswich in the 1978 FA Cup Final was tremendous. The demand for me to play well and score was just as great. Arsenal were the hottest favourites since Leeds took on Second Division Sunderland and, after two previous disappointments, I needed to be a Wembley winner at last. Before the final week I thought we would win easily but on the great day I wasn't confident.

I should have gone into hospital five months earlier for a cartilage operation and my left knee was definitely suspect. Other Arsenal players were struggling with injuries and it made us laugh when Ipswich manager Bobby Robson kept complaining of having an injury-hit squad.

Ipswich, of course, fielded their strongest side, while Liam Brady, possibly skipper Pat Rice, and I should not have taken the gamble. We also had a few problems in the dressing room that week and, in the end, Wembley again turned into a nightmare for me.

My left knee locked about twenty times and the Ipswich players kept staring in amazement as I stopped to loosen the joints. Injuries always seem worse when you are losing and there was no doubt about the result as Ipswich grew in confidence in the second half.

They won with Roger Osborne's goal and the familiar sick feeling spread up from my stomach the moment the final whistle blew. My heart went out to the young players but inside I felt sorry for myself. The dressing room was just like before and it was only Pat Rice's vow to 'Win it next season' that broke the silence. The players seemed to respond to that, although I couldn't help feeling that fate wouldn't allow me a fourth Wembley final.

How could an Arsenal team of Pat Jennings, Pat Rice, David O'Leary, Willie Young, Sammy Nelson, Alan Hudson, David Price, Liam Brady, Frank Stapleton, me and Alan Sunderland lose to Ipswich? So much talent ... if only Brady had been completely fit, if only my knee had stood up, if only, if only ....

I was slaughtered afterwards in the press and labelled the 'Wembley loser' and 'Superflop'. I expected it, but criticism has never worried me throughout my career. I like to pride myself on being big enough to take what anyone can throw at me. Like all footballers I bask in the glory of success and I accept criticism as part of the ball game. My family, close friends and I knew why I hadn't done well and that was good enough for me. I am not offering my knee now as an open excuse, I elected to play and paid the penalty.

In a strange way my three Wembley defeats helped me accept the ultimate setback when I was forced to retire. At the time losing in a Cup Final seems the worst possible thing that can happen. You don't think you can cope with anything else. Then when you are told you must give up your profession, losing football matches seems rather a small incident in your memory. It did make me determined to kick back and make something of my life.

I am just pleased to have been given the opportunity to play in a final and enjoy the atmosphere three times over. If I had won all three and scored goals I would probably have ended up a completely different person.

Pat Rice kept to his word and led Arsenal back to Wembley a year later, and this time victory came over Manchester United in a superb five-goal final. I was in the squad but not fit enough to play, I thought I was probably two weeks away from full match fitness. I sat on the bench alongside Don Howe, Terry Neill, Fred Street and substitute Steve Walford and although I did my share of shouting I felt like an outsider.

It is strange that in our national stadium, Wembley have not arranged better seating for the two clubs on Cup Final day.

There are no dugouts, only benches, and both sets of managers and coaches are sitting on top of each other. There are no secrets, and messages and tactics are passed around and shouted out in full hearing of the opposition. When a substitute is sent on his instructions are made very public.

You live the ecstasy of goals and agony of defeat in full view of your enemy. When Alan Sunderland scored Arsenal's last-minute winner in a memorable finish we danced in celebration right on top of Dave Sexton. Surely Wembley can do better than that?

There is definitely not the same atmosphere surrounding the League Cup Final although in 1976, when Newcastle returned to Wembley just two years after our disastrous performance against Liverpool, we were desperate to win for our supporters. Alan Kennedy, Pat Howard, Tommy Cassidy and I were the only players left in the side who lost to Liverpool, but the others knew how important it was for Newcastle to beat Manchester City on 28 February.

Peter Barnes put City ahead with an early goal but we fought back and Cassidy and I combined for Alan Gowling to equalize. At half time we thought we were going to do it, only for Dennis Tueart to win the game for City with his now famous scissor-kick goal directly after the interval. The style in which Tueart took his goal was a killer for us and although we fought hard Newcastle lost once more at Wembley. We were not humiliated again, but the feeling of defeat is the same.

Part of the build-up to Wembley for every club includes an endless list of requests from television, newspapers, radio, recording studios and companies who want their name linked with the Cup finalists. It is an accepted part of the razzmatazz and the money the players earn from these stunts is dropped into the same piggy bank and shared amongst the first team squad. It is called the Players' Pool.

A number of outsiders are very confused about pools. They believe they are wrong and that players should not be allowed to earn great sums of money on top of their already alleged inflated salaries.

The first answer I will give is that the most I have collected from the four pools I have been involved with is £850 after Newcastle's defeat by Liverpool.

Members of the public have got to appreciate that a footballer's career span is short and therefore his life as a money earner is restricted to the years that he stays at the top. The Cup Final represents the biggest day of his life and perhaps his only chance to collect some fringe benefits from the game. Who would begrudge someone like Roger Osborne, Ipswich's goal-scoring hero against Arsenal, a share of an extra pay-out? He will probably never play in a Wembley Cup Final again in his life. If a carpenter is asked to make something outside his normal working hours he expects payment. The same principle applies to a footballer at Wembley.

I have always thought that football clubs and newspapers should work closely with one another and that includes the final week before Wembley. Footballers who give interviews and pose for photographs for nothing throughout their careers should not suddenly ask for money when the request is small. But I believe a payment should be made if the work involves a day at a studio or a newspaper feature or picture special.

Pools often develop into more trouble than they are worth and problems always arise when the money is declared to the tax man. I have been in a team when every member of the squad wrote a different figure down on his tax form. One player said he was paid £400 and spent £388 in expenses. The person or company running the pool of course has to declare the correct figures and it doesn't take an Inland Revenue clerk long to work out another tax dodge.

I feel far more strongly about how players are treated by people actually inside the game. After Newcastle's defeat by Liverpool a special payment of £10.50 appeared in my next pay packet. It turned out to be my fee for the television rights. It was an insulting payment from one of the biggest live televised sporting events in Britain and another example of how players are treated in this country. The Football Association sells recordings of the Cup Final all over the world, the game is used as a big source of income, and yet all the Liverpool and Newcastle players received was £10.50 from TV rights!

I don't know if they think that players should just sit back and accept everything they are told and given, but the FA Cup Final remains one of the big mysteries of football to me. Where does all the money go, who gets it? The 22 players should be the most important people at Wembley on Cup Final Saturday and yet they are lost in the middle of big business operations and by three o'clock sport almost takes second place. There is too much pressure to win, too much money at stake for the Cup Final to always live up to its incredible build-up.

One man's name always crops up at Cup Final time, and that's Stan Flashman, 'Fat Stan', king of the ticket touts and enemy of the public. Stan is criticized every year and painted as a crook, and yet all he is doing is providing a service. He is a legitimate business man and pays his tax.

The law of the Football Association states that no-one in the game should sell Cup Final tickets that have been distributed to them. It does not say anything about people buying those tickets. Everyone knows that Stan's sources are numerous within football and it is those men who should be punished. He sells his tickets at inflated prices, but he sells them at the asking price he knows he can get. If there was not one ticket on the black market, true supporters would still go without.

Stan is never praised for the work he does within the game or appreciated for what he does for footballers all over the country. He is continually being asked to sit on players' testimonial committees and raise money for certain charities. They are jobs that often leave him out of pocket. It makes me angry when someone is condemned out of hand for providing his customers with a service.

The fact that he is known as 'Fat Stan' and his name is Flashman obviously doesn't help him. If he was plain Peter Brown and half the size, he would go about his business unrecognized and probably double his income. And don't forget there are a lot of little Stan Flashmans running around!

12

Ramsey and Mercer

Alf Ramsey always had a polite, respectful way of talking to his players and our brief meeting on Friday, 19 May 1972 was no exception. 'Malcolm, I would like you to play for England tomorrow.'

There was not a trace of emotion on the England manager's face and although I wanted to stand on my head and shout for joy I just replied: 'Thank you Alf, I will not let you down'.

My first cap at 22, England versus Wales at Ninian Park in the Home International championship. I had only been at Newcastle a year, and was still learning the trade of centre forward, and yet I was being asked to play for England. Asked, I would have paid Alf to have picked me.

There are certain memories that stay with you for ever. Things that are tucked away at the back of your mind that bring a smile to your face when they drift unexpectedly into focus. Making your debut for your country is one of those things.

It is a special occasion for you alone. There is not the crazy build up of a Cup Final and there are no team-mates to share the excitement. So you drink the atmosphere in, listening to the manager and staying silent when senior players voice opinions in the dressing room.

I played for England under three managers, Alf, Joe Mercer and Don Revie and there is no doubt in my mind that I would have won more than my fourteen caps and scored more than six goals if Ramsey had stayed in control.

Dear old Joe Mercer was a romantic interlude between Ramsey and Revie and all the players respected and fought for Joe, as they did for Alf.

Revie was something different. The Leeds manager, the obvious choice after his success at Elland Road, moved into

Lancaster Gate with his motivation of pennies and pressure. Like many players I was discarded without warning or feeling and I will never forgive the man for what he didn't do for English football.

Revie lost the respect of some of his players and when that happens you might as well hold your hands up and say: 'I'm sorry, I have failed'. Respect is always something Alf received from his England men; even today there is not one of us who would say a word against him.

Before I played for England I laughed when I read how players reacted when they pulled on the white shirt. 'It makes you proud', they would say. Well, that is just how I felt, proud to be playing for England in this team boasting so much skill and experience: Gordon Banks (Stoke City), Paul Madeley (Leeds), Roy McFarland (Derby), Bobby Moore (West Ham), Emlyn Hughes (Liverpool), Peter Storey (Arsenal), Colin Bell (Manchester City), Norman Hunter (Leeds), Mike Summerbee (Manchester City), Rodney Marsh (Manchester City), and me.

Emlyn Hughes moved up from full back to put us ahead but at half time I was worried about the way Rodney Marsh and I were combining. I made a lot of runs down the left and all it needed from Rodney was a through ball and I would have been clear.

At least five times I screamed at Rodney to release the ball and each time it went out to the right for his Manchester City team-mate Mike Summerbee. 'What the hell's going on?' I asked in the dressing room. 'I have been screaming at you to put me through.'

'Sorry pal', he answered. 'But you're running on my deaf side.' To this day I don't know if I had fallen for Rodney's unique sense of humour or if he was really telling me that the deafness in his left ear affected his performance.

I never thought Rodney took the game seriously enough and he always seemed to find time for a laugh on the pitch. It is a tragedy that, like so many skilful players in my era, he only won a handful of caps.

He was superbly graceful for a big man and had so much skill and power when it mattered. He could have become one of the real greats with a change of attitude. Rodney could make a manager either dance with delight or shake his head in frustration. I was sitting on the bench at Hampden Park once when Alf put his hands in the air and shouted: 'Will someone get that clown off?'

After we had beaten Wales 3-0 I played for the first time at Wembley against Northern Ireland four days later. I was enjoying the atmosphere, just being inside the big dressing room, everything that goes with Wembley, when my night was ruined by Denis Follows, who was then secretary of the Football Association.

All the England kit is laid out in team order from one to eleven and I was changing next to Rodney when Follows began moving around the dressing room shaking hands. 'How are you, nice to see you again, have a good game tonight, hello Rodney ...' and then he came to me, 'Hello, young man, and who are you?'

I was demoralized, thought: 'Who am I? I'm only England's centre forward at Wembley.' I managed to whisper an embarrassed 'I'm Malcolm Macdonald'. The night went from bad to worse when I was substituted by Martin Chivers of Spurs, and Terry Neill, then Hull City's player-manager, scored the only goal of the game for Northern Ireland.

Alf Ramsey hated the Scots and they, in turn, despised him. His team talks before a Scotland international were always filled with that little extra emotion, that little extra motivation. 'You know I hate them', he would start. 'If you don't want to beat them for yourselves, go out and beat them for me. Please.'

We never feared anyone under Alf. He always made us think we were the best team in the world. 'You are England players and we are the best', he would say. 'The rest of the world respects us, they want to beat us. Don't let them.'

The coach journey to Hampden Park for the international against Scotland is like trying to pass through a frenzied picket line. There are drunken Scots everywhere. Inside the England coach it was always the same, Alf sat up front, tight-lipped and serious, while little Alan Ball bounced around on the back seat, making faces and shaking his fists at the Scots fans.

On one particular occasion our coach was inching along to the main entrance and the Jock supporters were giving us their official welcome. That meant as the coach moved along they lifted up their kilts and urinated down the side of the bus. One big Scot, drunk out of his brains and holding a can of McEwans in each hand, was hitting the side of the coach with his head as he rocked to and fro. His eyes were closed as he muttered: 'English bastards'. The trouble was he didn't open his eyes once as the coach moved slowly on and he fell flat on his face, kilt over

his head and McEwans still held tightly … unconscious! 'Bally'
danced with delight. He hated the Scots as much as Alf.

I loved playing in the same side as 'Bally'. He was a player's
dream, driving you on for 90 minutes in his little chirpy voice,
always supporting, always giving just the right pass. So many
crowds all over the world hated the little man but they couldn't
help but respect him.

He was just one of the players Revie discarded too soon. Even
though Alan didn't rate England's new manager or respect him,
he would have died for England in a Revie side. Alan was never
given an official reason why he was thrown out but I believe
Revie looked on him as a threat to his position, someone who saw
right through his many false ways.

Consistency is an over-used word in football today but it was
Alf Ramsey's greatest quality during his career as England
manager. He never changed from the moment I first met him to
the day of his last international, away to Portugal on 3 April
1974. Rather like Alec Stock, he commanded respect and always
treated the players like men. If you were punished by Alf it hurt
him to do it but it meant you always deserved the reprimand.

A knock on the front door of my Flitwick home by a Luton
policeman sent me rushing to my first meeting with Alf. He had
sent out an SOS for me to join up with his England Under 23
squad at Heathrow and the FA had contacted my local police
station for help. It was nine o'clock in the morning when the
bobby told Julie her husband was wanted at London Airport. I
just made the flight and Alf was waiting in the departure lounge.
It was me who should have been pleased but Alf genuinely
seemed delighted to see me. He shook hands and he said:
'Malcolm, I can't thank you enough for coming at such short
notice. I am very grateful.'

He actually seemed to mean it and I later discovered that he
always went out of his way to thank his players personally at the
end of each international. 'Thank you very much for helping
me' was his message to each player. There was no indication that
you were going to be selected again, not even to Bobby Moore,
only a warm handshake, and a smile.

When the knives went into Alf and the pressure mounted over
his future as England manager he never allowed the players to
sense there was anything wrong. Whatever bitterness he felt
towards his enemies, he was too much of a gentleman to voice his

true opinions in public, and the team were treated in exactly the same way. He cushioned all the troubles.

In Portugal the press requested a meeting with the players and Alf came to us and asked if we were keen. 'Bally' said he wasn't and the rest of us agreed. We didn't think it would achieve anything in the middle of preparing for an international. On the flight home I discovered that Alf had told the press boys that he was against any meeting with the side. That was typical of Alf Ramsey, he didn't allow his players to be exposed to criticism ever.

I have only happy memories of playing under Alf and I am proud that I was in this line-up, the last team he selected as England manager: Phil Parkes (Queen's Park Rangers), David Nish (Derby), Dave Watson (Sunderland), Colin Todd (Derby), Mike Pejic (Stoke), Martin Dobson (Burnley), Trevor Brooking (West Ham), Martin Peters (Spurs), Stan Bowles (Queen's Park Rangers), Mike Channon (Southampton), and me. It was a strange-looking side for Alf but we managed to draw 0-0.

After he was sacked there was no public reaction from Ramsey. The players, while wanting to say something on his behalf, respected his decision to stay silent. It is ironic that one of Alf's biggest problems during his reign was the release of players from club commitments and Revie's Leeds were the main culprits. You would have thought that Leeds fought wars every Saturday afternoon the number of times Revie pulled his players out of England squads. And then when he became Alf's permanent successor he announced: 'I hope to have full co-operation from club managers over the release of players'.

I don't think the men who sit at Lancaster Gate and decide who should manage England fully appreciate what a great job for English football Alf Ramsey did. Despite the fact that he would have done the job for nothing, he was paid peanuts and worked under a great deal of non-co-operation pressure.

The players he picked paid their own small tribute when only twenty of the 102 men who won caps under Alf failed to arrive at a special testimonial dinner. Others travelled from all over Britain to be part of Alf's big night. I don't think many of us would cross the road to be at a similar function for Don Revie.

The Football Association couldn't have made a better choice for England's caretaker manager than Joe Mercer. He had a marvellous public image, a love for the game and a real feeling for players. He knew he only had the job for a few matches and he went out to enjoy himself. Joe always had a smile on his face and that is the way we played under him. It was impossible not to like Joe Mercer.

He introduced unlikely candidates like Leicester's Frank Worthington and Keith Weller to international football and they responded with goals and outstanding performances.

Mercer's record as England manager was good. He picked up the pieces after Alf and lost only one, against Scotland at Hampden Park, in seven internationals. It included an unbeaten tour in June 1974 behind the Iron Curtain when we drew with East Germany in Leipzig, beat Bulgaria 1-0 in Sofia and drew against Yugoslavia in Belgrade.

Joe was in a lot of pain with a back injury on that tour and it became so bad during the night that at times he couldn't sleep unless he was sitting upright in a hard-backed chair. Yet every morning he was up bright and early greeting us cheerfully at breakfast. Like Alf, he refused to allow his problems to be seen by the players.

It was a shame therefore that in Yugoslavia Joe should have to be involved with an international incident that was one of the ugliest experienced by England anywhere in the world — the day Kevin Keegan was beaten up and then held by Yugoslav airport guards.

The FA chartered a plane for the entire tour but for some unknown reason we had to travel by Bulgarian Airways into Yugoslavia. Frank Worthington had beaten Bulgaria with his second goal in four internationals, and because we only had four hours' sleep after the game it was a very tired England party that trooped into Yugoslavia.

Kevin Keegan, who had only just forced his way into the England side at that stage, slept throughout the entire flight and he was still in a semi-conscious state as we waited for our cases. Kevin sat on the side of the conveyor belt, clutching some valuable cut glass he had bought in East Germany, and didn't seem at all interested when Liverpool full back Alec Lindsey did an Irish jig behind him on the belt. It was just a silly prank and when someone in the distance shouted at Alec to get off the incident was forgotten.

Suddenly two armed guards appeared from nowhere, grabbed Kevin so roughly that he dropped his glass and watched in horror as it smashed all over the floor, and dragged him into a back office. We looked on in amazement as Kevin was man-handled, but it happened so quickly he disappeared before any of us could react to help him. It is not the kind of treatment you expect from a country hosting an official party from England.

No sooner had the office door slammed shut than we heard the sickening thud of punches thrown and Kevin crying out in pain. It was an unreal situation and it happened in a matter of seconds. Anyone's immediate reaction is to help a friend and about eight of us raced forward to storm the small office. We were stopped in our tracks by the barrel of a gun pointing straight at us. I have never backed away from a fight in my life. But this was different, you can't argue with a revolver or the guard standing behind it. He didn't say a word but the message was clear: 'One more step nearer and I will fire'.

A terrible feeling of panic and helplessness spread through the England players and we just ran around the airport trying to find an FA official or an elder statesman. There was an incredible lack of concern about Kevin's wellbeing. I remember shouting at someone 'Look, one of your players is being held captive. Do something about it.'

I was furious, how could England be treated this way? It was intimidation of the highest degree and all the players were adamant: 'We are definitely not playing against Yugoslavia'. The entire squad wanted to go home there and then.

We desperately needed someone in authority to take charge of the situation. There just wasn't anyone from our party or the other side who seemed capable of accepting the responsibility and after much discussion and more threats we were persuaded to leave Kevin behind and go to our hotel. At this stage no-one even knew why Keegan had been whisked off.

An evening as guests of the Ambassador was the last thing in the world we wanted to do although it did eventually speed Kevin's release. No-one accepted the Ambassador's explanation but he said there had been a misunderstanding at the airport. 'You were all casually dressed, they thought you were trouble-makers', he said. I still don't see how somebody's being casually dressed gives anyone the right to go around fighting and waving a gun.

The Ambassador even left us with another ultimatum: 'You must play the game', he warned, 'otherwise there will be an international incident' I thought there already had been.

Kevin was eventually set free after spending the entire day locked up at the airport and, after more talks between the players, we reluctantly agreed to play the match. There was no way we were going to lose and there was a happy ending for Kevin as he scored our second goal in a 2-2 draw. It still remains one of the sweetest goals of his magnificent England career.

In the final minutes I had a chance to get the result we all desperately wanted when Alec Lindsey put me clear of their defence with a great through ball from the halfway line. I accelerated into the area and had only the goalkeeper to beat. It was a simple chance, a sitter, I should have scored. Instead I pushed my shot too wide and watched in horror as the ball went the wrong side of a post. I have never worried about missing chances but I wished I had scored on that occasion. I wanted to score for Kevin, for the rest of the team and to put two fingers up at the Yugoslavs.

On an earlier England tour, this time to Russia, another amazing incident almost ended with Roy McFarland, David Nish, Peter Shilton and me being left behind.

One night after we had finished playing cards, we discovered that the door to the hotel room was locked from the outside. A frantic phone call to the maid didn't get us out, for she insisted it was our problem. Another phone call, this time to the night manager, with the demand: 'You have got to do something, the door won't open from the inside or outside and our plane for Italy leaves in five hours'.

A few minutes later and without any warning there was a tremendous crash. We stood back and watched in amazement as the wood splintered and a huge hole appeared in the door. A man outside had just smashed it down with an axe! We climbed through the gaping hole in the door, but the Russians wouldn't return our passports until we had paid for the damage. I always wondered what Alf would have done if he had been locked in.

It was his complete control of situations and his uncanny knack of putting people in their place that will always stick in my memory.

During my first match under his control, the Under 23 International against Scotland at Hampden Park, he came up to me during training. I had been watching him closely moving around the other players and wondered what instructions he was giving. 'Malcolm, I would like to thank you again for joining us at such short notice and although I can't include you in the team tomorrow, would you like to be one of the substitutes?'

Would I like to be a sub? He must have been kidding; 24 hours earlier I had been sitting at home at Flitwick. 'I would love to sub, Alf', I said. 'And don't worry, I will be in your side soon, I have got time on my side.'

He looked at me straight in the eyes and replied, 'Malcolm, you may or may not be in my side one day, but you will never have time on your side'.

How right he was.

13

Don Revie

It doesn't take a man long to know whether he likes someone. The feeling of friendship and respect usually grows from a first meeting. You agree about the same things, laugh at similar jokes. Friends are hand-picked, carefully selected as people to socialize with and turn to when you have problems.

With England football squads you don't get a choice. They represent a complete cross-section of men thrown together from all corners of the country to live under the same roof. A natural bond is formed because at that particular time you are all selected as the best footballers in England, but a player can win 25 caps and still not meet a man he would like to call a good friend.

The manager, therefore, is the most important person at any England get-together. He is the father figure, the man to knit the whole operation together. He must gain the respect of the players during training as well as on and off the field and not fall out with anyone. He must motivate and keep the players interested. For four days he is the most important man in English football.

Don Revie was a walking disaster for our national game. We wasted four years while he was in control. And I am not putting the boot in just because Revie dumped me on the international scrapheap when, I believe, I was at my goalscoring peak. I have a deep feeling for England and the way I channel my efforts and emotions back are through football. If I had not won a single England cap my feeling of disgust towards Don Revie would be the same.

If you wanted games of bingo or thick complicated dossiers to frighten you into making mistakes, and money motivation, then Don Revie was your man.

There was no pride or passion in his voice behind the locked dressing-room door. He would make every opposition sound like world champions; instead of walking out feeling ten feet tall, I began every match under Don Revie trying to build myself up.

I don't think Revie appreciated what playing for England meant to most of the men he inherited. People like Alan Ball are passionately patriotic and we would all have gone out and fought for our country for nothing. Of course it is rewarding to be paid well for doing something you only usually dream about, but Revie would promise us pound notes and expect us to respond.

'Be successful with me and I will make you rich', he said to us before important matches. 'You are the best in the country. I will make you the best paid. Win today and I will get you more.' It was an obsession with him.

We all appreciated how he increased the match fees from £50 to £100 for a draw and from £100 to £200 for a win, but his attitude was wrong. With every team talk about money Don Revie lost a little more respect from the established members of the squad.

If someone had said to me at the start of my career: one day you are going to score five goals for England in an international at Wembley, I would have paid him a fortune to make it come true. That night on 16 April 1975 against Cyprus remains one of my greatest memories. Scoring goals for England meant more to me than anything Don Revie could understand.

He was also petrified of losing. The thought of failure sent waves of panic surging through him and, naturally, he passed it on to us. His dossiers, huge complicated folders of information on the opposition, reflected his make-up. There was never anything about us in the dossiers, only how good the opposition could be, paragraphs on players none of us had ever heard of.

The description of what might happen during the game were pure science fiction. My main job was supposed to be scoring goals but all I read was 'No. 5 and No. 6 are good players and will receive cover from No. 3. Be careful when you move out to the wing because No. 11 might drop back in support.' We were supposed to read them twice at bedtime. Instead they went straight in the wastepaper bin.

Sometimes the dossiers covered fifteen different opposing players and then, when you checked the names in the dressing room before the game, only five were playing.

Before we went out against Cyprus Revie produced a classic. 'Cyprus are at war at home', he said. 'They will probably be mad.' He made them sound better than West Germany and I fully expected to see a few tanks and armed soldiers lined up in front of their goal.

Why didn't he build us up instead? 'Let's go and show this bunch of upstarts how to play. We are England, they shouldn't be on the same pitch as us. We can score ten tonight.' That is all Don needed to have said.

I always watched other players during team meetings, half time talks and pre-match discussions. I liked to see how they reacted; it was always a reliable way of telling how they were going to respond. Some of the newcomers seemed impressed. Others like Alan Ball and Colin Bell just shook their heads in amazement.

Revie of course had his good points. He was a very thorough man, planning down to the last detail travel arrangements, hotel accommodation and menus for the team. Nothing was left to chance and he was also a very puritanical person in his beliefs. He didn't like his players misbehaving themselves at home or abroad and once he told us: 'You should go down on your hands and knees every night and thank God, like I do, for giving you such a good life'. He actually expected us to pray at night and then hop into bed and read his dossiers!

It was Alan Ball, whom Revie had made skipper one match earlier — a 2-0 friendly victory over West Germany at Wembley — who produced the motivation I needed before our European Championship match against Cyprus. In our hotel a few hours before kick-off Alan took me to one side and said: 'There is a goalscoring record to be broken tonight. You can do it. Cyprus are there for the taking.' Bally had done Revie's job. Simple motivation.

He kept driving me on during the game and after my first goal held up one finger and shouted: 'That's one, keep going'. He didn't say 'well done' or 'good goal' once, only holding up fingers to indicate how many more goals he wanted. After my hat-trick Kevin Keegan trotted over with this classic comment: 'Give someone else a chance, Mal, there are plenty of goals to go round'.

Only at the end of the game when the giant Wembley scoreboard lit up the message 'SuperMac 5 Cyprus 0' did Alan Ball come over to me with congratulations. He looked up at the sign and said: 'That is what this game is all about'. I had written my name into the record books and 'Bally' had pushed me there. My goals are the only five by any player in any post-war full international, and only the second five for England in the last 80 years, the previous man to do it being Willie Hall of Spurs in an international against Northern Ireland at Old Trafford. I will always treasure those goals and I remember them so well.

I knew in the first few minutes it was going to be my night when Ball and Hudson combined to send a free kick to the far post and I met it with the centre of my forehead to put it in the bottom corner. There is nothing better than scoring an early goal. From that moment I went after the record.

Kevin Keegan made the second with a run down the left and a low cross. Standing just six yards out, I leant back to volley the ball into the net, only to mis-hit it and watch it trickle into the corner with the goalkeeper going the wrong way.

It was the kind of goal you score when nothing goes wrong, and soon after half time Keegan again was involved in the build up to make my hat-trick. He sent over another cross and this time a downward header made it 3-0. Cyprus, who were not a good team, began to panic and I could sense they were losing all their defensive organization.

Dave Thomas of Queen's Park Rangers came on as substitute and he soon sent over a tremendous cross from the right that allowed me to head another goal. The service was so good from Thomas on the right and Keegan down the left that I couldn't fail to get on the end of chances. I even had a goal disallowed and hit the post.

Thomas destroyed their defence again with his speed and this time a near-post cross and a glancing header made it 5-0.

In the dressing room I was on cloud nine. I admit it, I had the match ball in my bag and just wanted to bask in the glory. Don Revie soon sent me crashing down to earth. 'The television and radio boys want to see you', he said. 'Don't worry about the fee, leave that to me.'

I couldn't believe my ears. I had just scored five goals for England and wanted to tell the world about it and Revie was talking about money again. 'Don't worry, Don', I said. 'I'd rather you didn't mention it.'

Revie had already scratched the gloss from my greatest night when BBC interviewer Tony Gubba rubbed it away completely. In the after-match interview he put this first question to me:

'Well, Malcolm, it has been a successful game for you, but what about the two you missed?'

Sorry, Tony, if I scored only from five out of seven chances I received.

The entire night went wrong from that moment. Some friends I had arranged to meet at a club in London didn't turn up and I sat there, sipping my beer and listening to other people's conversation. I heard someone mention the game and it seemed that everyone was celebrating England's five goals except the person who had scored them.

I slipped back to the team's hotel and altered my travel arrangements to the first flight back to Newcastle the following morning. Football can be a lonely game even for a hero!

We beat Cyprus away a month later and although Revie kept changing his side around he seemed to have got close to a good balanced team when we thrashed Scotland 5-1 at Wembley on 24 May 1975. I was not in the team but you couldn't argue with the way England played that day. Was this the start of a new era?

Revie then astounded everyone and broke Alan Ball's heart by dropping the captain without public reason. It was the last time 'Bally' ever got in an England squad.

We then stumbled on to Czechoslovakia and a disastrous 2-1 defeat in Bratislava that virtually knocked us out of the Championship. Revie picked me again and you could sense how uptight and scared of losing he was in the dressing room. He was like a caged tiger, never settling, moving around anxiously from player to player.

It was then that he proved to me just what kind of pressure he was under and how scared he was of failure. As we were getting changed, he invited me to take a pill from a little pot he was holding. 'What are they, Don?' I asked.

'Just something to park you up', he answered. 'Don't worry, they will not do you any harm.'

I am sure the pills were something innocuous like aspirins or Smarties but Revie seemed to believe that taking the pills would have some psychological effect. I didn't need 'perking'. I was playing for England in a vital European Championship game. No player needs a greater motivation than playing for his country. I have never needed anything to relax me or make me feel good and the last place I would experiment with strange pills was in the dressing room.

The first game against the Czechs was, ironically, abandoned because of fog and the pills were not handed round the following day when we lost. I'm sure none of the other players took one of Revie's pills, whatever they were, and he never produced them again.

I only played once more under Revie, in a 1-1 draw away to Portugal in Lisbon on 19 November 1975. I was substituted by Dave Thomas and had strong words for the England manager when I walked off: 'How can you expect me to play well with no service coming from midfield?' I told him. 'Surely we must play to our strengths?' He just told me to sit down and I was never picked again.

Goodbyes from Revie can be brutal, as Alan Ball discovered, and I was told officially that I was no longer wanted by England with a short, sharp *unsigned* letter from Revie.

The letter was sent to St James' Park and, like anyone, I sorted through my correspondence looking for the interesting envelopes and tossing aside the bills. The FA stamp caught my eye immediately and I tore it open expecting good news. Instead I was shocked and bitterly disappointed at what I read.

I have since thrown the letter away in disgust but I recall it said something like: 'Dear Malcolm, This is to say I will not be selecting you for future England squads....' Just like that, my international career finished in one cruel sentence.

And at the bottom of the short letter came the final twist of Revie's knife. He didn't even have the decency to sign it himself, there was just a typed message, signed in Mr Revie's absence.

I showed the letter to my Newcastle team-mates who were getting changed for training and they all agreed: what a dirty trick to play.

I have never seen Revie since and he didn't contact me to explain the real reasons why I was discarded. I don't know why he let me know like that and I would have preferred a phone call or a quiet chat the next time we bumped into each other. And if it had to be by letter, why didn't he wait until he had the time to at least sign it?

The way Revie tossed Ball aside was perhaps even a worse lesson in man-management. Ball had been Revie's captain but there was no warning before Alan received this impersonal letter from the England manager:

Dear Alan,
I hope you receive this letter before you read the morning papers, as I would like to thank you for all you have done for

the Football Association and me personally over the last season.

I have not selected you for the squad for the Switzerland match and I will be making Gerry Francis captain. I have not discarded you completely, and I only hope that you will, if recalled for any special match, play for me. I know this must come as a terrible blow, but I am letting you know first the complete position.

I hope that you soon get all your difficulties sorted out. If I can help you in any way I will be only too pleased to do so as you know.

Good luck for the future.

Revie then hit 'Bally' between the eyes by not signing the letter personally; like mine, it just said, 'Dictated by Mr. Revie and signed in his absence'. It was the worst possible way to say 'you're out' to a player who had given everything for his country. We are still waiting to find out the real reasons. Revie was wrong in most people's eyes over the handling of Alan Ball and I think it has been proved since that he dropped him too soon.

Ball is just one of the many players Revie didn't understand. I was another, and he never appeared to try and get through to Hudson. He seemed to look on us as a threat, a challenge to his leadership or to be frightened of us, to think other players would follow us instead of doing as they were told. That is a slur on our character and completely wrong. We were desperate to make England great again, probably more so than Revie himself.

It is impossible to treat all players the same and Revie should have taken more trouble getting to know individuals. Some of us are not angels, we like a drink, a laugh and a night out, but that does not mean to say we are challenging the manager. I never once broke a curfew or one of Revie's rules.

At Newcastle Joe Harvey preferred his players to stay in on a Thursday night but he knew that Terry Hibbitt always went to his local pub for a game of crib and a couple of pints. What was the point of stopping Terry? It would have broken his routine, unsettled him and probably affected his performance on Saturday. He would have lost respect for the manager.

Alan Ball and Alan Hudson played together for England only three times, against West Germany, and Cyprus twice. We won all three and they were both outstanding. So why drop them? I scored five goals in six internationals under Revie, so why drop me? I am not the best footballer that has ever played for my country, but I scored goals and I would have got a lot more for England.

It is no coincidence that the names of Alan Ball and Alan Hudson crop up a lot in this book. They are there as friends, as players I respect and as perfect examples of the wrongs and rights in football. Too many people will no doubt package the three of us together and dismiss us as arrogant footballers with a chip on our shoulders. If that is the case, then you are all as guilty as Don Revie.

There have been and will be many more players like Ball and Hudson who have been misunderstood and badly treated. It is a pity that 'Bally' didn't find Southampton manager Lawrie McMenemy earlier in his career, or have been able to take Sir Alf Ramsey into the First Division with him.

English football never saw the best of Alan Hudson and for that he can blame himself and the men who didn't try or know how to use a great talent.

Just because the three of us speak our minds and refuse to be treated like schoolboys, it doesn't mean to say we enjoy entering into controversy. We are not trying to prove we are better than the manager or on a different plane to anyone else in the game.

I am the first to admit that I have made hundreds of mistakes and often said the wrong thing at the wrong time. A lot of them were at Newcastle when I was at the peak of my career and in the public eye every single day. But Joe Harvey didn't react badly or expose my errors; he knew my value to the team and put that before anything else. It is understanding and respect that a footballer most needs with his manager.

There were many friends I could have used instead of Ball and Hudson. But they were involved in incidents relevant to my story and the perfect examples of the side of football the public don't appreciate.

Ball, Hudson and I have an image in football that is not perfect, but would it have been any better if we had stayed silent and accepted all the things we knew that were wrong? I know I would never have had peace of mind.

Being picked for England is coupled with the special thrill of playing at Wembley Stadium. It is the ambition of most of the players in the world to play there and once you're out in the middle there is no doubt that it is a magnificent experience. The trouble is getting there and I'm afraid the access to the stadium and the facilities inside are some of the worst in world football.

The Football Association don't even own England's home ground, and surely it is time we built a new complex to cater for every sport played at national level in this country? It would prevent degrading situations arising like the FA having to ask if England can train on the pitch before an international.

I have always thought that an ideal site for a new project would be by the National Conference Centre in Birmingham. The motorway access is good and there is an airport close enough to offer reasonable service for supporters. I would like to see it shared by the FA, Rugby Union, the Amateur Athletic Association and an indoor complex opened seven days a week for members of the public. The powers that be will no doubt scream 'The cost is too high', but it could be done if we used the profits from the next twenty Cup Finals.

The road access to Wembley is so bad that the England coach would never get there on time for kick-off if it wasn't for the bravery of the police motorbike escort. He takes the coach driver through impossible traffic jams, accelerating into small gaps and just holding up his hand in front of oncoming cars. Before the Cyprus international, the coach got stuck on a muddy bank as we tried another short cut and it was just a question of all hands on deck. You should have seen the expression on the faces of passing strangers as England's million-pound footballers strained muscles and limbs to push the coach out of the mud!

On another occasion Julie and I had an important date to keep in the City and it meant a quick getaway from Wembley. I wasn't playing and, after collecting my bag from the dressing room, we were in our car twenty minutes after the final whistle. One-and-a-quarter hours later we were still trapped in the car park.

It made me realize just how difficult watching football at Wembley is. I don't know how regular supporters have put up with it for so long. It is amazing, and a tribute to their patriotism, that England are nearly always watched by capacity crowds.

14

A funny thing happened to me...

I have always thought that Eric Morecambe, the professional comedian, and Harry Haslam, the amateur, would make a great double act on television. They share the same sense of humour. No, not Luton Town!

It usually involves taking the mickey out of someone else and when Harry was manager and Eric a director at Kenilworth Road it was impossible not to be a target of two of the funniest men in football.

I dedicate this chapter to them both and relate with side-splitting memories some of the hilarious incidents that have happened to me over the last ten years.

* * *

When Harry was in charge at Tonbridge he gave a trial to a young Welsh player in an away match at Trowbridge. Because of travelling difficulties the kid didn't arrive until late on Friday night and Harry told him to go straight off to bed. He gave him the address of an elderly couple and said: 'The front door will be open, go straight in and yours is the front bedroom upstairs'.

The coach went round to pick him up the next morning at the crack of dawn and, as planned, the driver gave two hoots on the horn. There was not a soul around. We all watched as Harry got out and stood beneath the bedroom window. 'Come on, lad, we haven't got all day', he shouted.

With that a window opened five doors along and the Welsh lad popped his head out. He had slept in No. 52 instead of 42. To this day the club don't know whose house — or bed — he used!

* * *

Former Geordie favourite Len Shackleton never rated my goalscoring partner at Newcastle, John Tudor. Writing in the *Sunday People* newspaper, he always gave John only four marks out of ten. Whatever John did, Len would never give him more than four.

In one particular match Tudor was magnificent. He scored twice, completely dominated the game and received a standing ovation at the end of the match. Surely Len would give him more than four this time? He did. Five.

* * *

Harry Haslam once produced a superb defence at a disciplinary hearing for one of his Tonbridge players. Malcolm

Pyke, who stuttered badly, was sent off for calling the referee a bastard. Harry immediately ordered a personal hearing and decided to represent Pyke himself.

Malcolm never stuttered on the pitch, as he lost himself in the game. But as soon as the final whistle blew his problem returned and he just couldn't cope with pressure and embarrassing situations.

Harry knew that he would be uptight once they got inside for the hearing. 'I would like to ask just two questions', Harry told the chairman. 'One to the match referee and one to Mr Pyke.'

After the referee explained why Pyke had been sent off, Harry asked his second question: 'Malcolm, tell the committee what you called the referee'.

Malcolm took a deep breath and said: 'I called him a b-b-b-b ...' — case dismissed!

*   *   *

After Luton had clinched promotion to the Second Division by drawing 0-0 at Mansfield, the entire squad raced back down the M1 to celebrate at Caesar's Palace Night Club.

I was driving home after the party when a police squad car stopped me and ordered me into the back seat for a breath test. 'I'm Malcolm Macdonald', I said, trying desperately not to slur my words. 'I play for Luton and we won promotion tonight.'

It didn't seem to make much impression and so I pressed on boldly. 'The chairman of the club knows the chief constable and the manager is a best friend of your super.'

The policeman just shook his head and said: 'It's no good, mate, I'm a Watford supporter.'

Fortunately I passed the test.

*   *   *

When your club reaches the Cup Final every player is bombarded with requests for tickets. They come from strangers, relatives you haven't seen for years, the milkman and people who just stop you in the street.

I think the best begging letter I ever received came after Newcastle had won through to the 1974 FA Cup Final against Liverpool. It just said simply: 'I was conceived while my mother waited in a Cup Final queue, surely I am entitled to a ticket?'

*   *   *

Harry Haslam loved a laugh and mixing with the lads, but he
was a stickler for discipline and was clearly upset when one of his
Tonbridge players turned up late for a game. No-one could
understand why Harry didn't say anything and just let the
incident pass.

When we collected our next wage packets the player who had
been late found a watch in his envelope and his money docked by
£5.

'What's this?' 'I don't want a watch', demanded the player.

'Oh yes, you do', Harry said. 'Now you will never be late
again.'

* * *

Newcastle manager Gordon Lee once burst into our dressing
room after training and said: 'Is Aidan McCaffrey Irish?' No,
boss. 'Are his parents Irish?' No, boss. 'How dare he have a name

like McCaffrey and not be Irish?' Apparently Lee wanted to recommend Aidan for the Eire international squad.

'Steady on, Gordon', I said. 'My name is Malcolm Macdonald and you can't get more English than me.'

Lee snapped back: 'You should never be allowed to play for England with a Scottish name like Macdonald'.

By this time the whole dressing room was in hysterics and Tommy Cassidy sent Lee storming out of the door when he said: 'Excuse me, boss, but are you Chinese?'

*   *   *

In 1967 Tonbridge played Folkestone in the Kent FA Cup Final and I was picked to play in the second leg at outside left.

We were told to meet at the Angel pub where a coach would take us to Folkestone. Transport let me down but to my relief the coach was still there when I rushed into the pub forecourt.

There was no-one around but I thought they were all inside having coffee and so I climbed aboard, said hello to the driver, and settled down in the front seat. I became worried as the minutes ticked by and then suddenly 30 blokes came out of the pub, got into the coach and we started to move off.

'Wait a minute, this is the Tonbridge football coach and we are going to Folkestone', I shouted.

'No it isn't, mate', a gruff voice said behind me. 'This is the Miners' Welfare outing and we are going for a few beers.'

I dashed to the station, but the first train to Folkestone would not have got me there in time for kick-off. So it was a very disappointed young man who trooped off home again. I never played in another Cup Final until seven years later at Wembley.

*   *   *

Arsenal manager Terry Neill once caught the full impact of Harry Haslam's wit and sharp tongue. The three of us were discussing football and Terry turned the conversation around to management. Harry has always been proud of his days at Tonbridge when he had to do every job possible and he soon stopped Terry in his tracks. Harry leant across the table and said: 'Terry, you'll never be a complete manager until you know where every bog on the ground is'.

*   *   *

In a Southern League match for Tonbridge at Dartford a bloke at the back of the stands had a terrible go at me throughout the first half. He shouted at me, moaned at every tackle and made life very miserable.

As we came off at half time I said to Harry: 'Can't we do something about that idiot?' Harry just jumped over the fence that surrounded the pitch, raced up the steps and chased the man out of the ground.

After the game the Dartford chairman came into our dressing room looking for Harry. 'Mr Haslam', he said, 'The next time you chase someone out of the ground would you please make sure it is not one of my directors?'

Harry came to my rescue again at Romford. Two people sitting on the fence moaned about my tackling and at half time Harry picked up a bucket of water and just threw it over them. That's what I call a loyal manager.

* * *

Luton were playing in a game we had to win but the match was in doubt because it had been raining all night and Kenilworth Road was very boggy.

Manager Alec Stock arrived at 7.30 in the morning, put his boots on and walked out to groundsman Eddie Hartley, who had already been working on the pitch for two hours. 'What's it like?' Alec asked.

'It will be OK, Mr Stock,' Eddie replied. 'We have worked hard on it.'

Stock then ordered Hartley to flood the entire ground. 'Get the hoses on it', he demanded. 'I don't want the game on.' Eddie spent the next hour setting up sprinklers, hoses and a human chain of buckets.

He reported to Alec that his staff were ready, only for Stock to change his mind. 'I have been thinking', he said. 'I know we can beat them, let's play after all.'

The buckets were emptied and everything put away when Stock strode out and ordered the pitch to be flooded again. It happened three times before Alec actually decided to let the game take place.

We beat Doncaster 4-2 and Hartley was telling me the crazy happenings of the morning over a beer when Alec strode up and said: 'Malcolm, you are talking to someone who has no confidence in the team. I'm surprised at you, Eddie, not wanting to play the game!'

* * *

I have always been able to sprint quickly and when I was at Newcastle a race was organized between me and a British professional sprint champion. It was held in the middle of an athletics meeting at Gateshead and the betting was heavy amongst the big crowd.

The best price you could get on me was 6-4 and he was always firm favourite. Although he gave me a five-metre start I wanted to win. My reputation was at stake. I left the blocks like a train and felt really good. Suddenly I heard his feet behind me and then his breath as he drew up alongside. He was moving like a bomb.

My chest went out, I gritted my teeth and thought to myself: 'You're not going to beat me'. I just got the verdict on the line by five inches. 'Well done, Malcolm', he said afterwards. 'A great race.'

After I had changed I popped my head round his dressing room door to ask him for a drink and caught him stuffing ten-pound notes into his pockets. A mate of his had £400 on me at 6-4 to win. 'Don't complain,' he said with a grin. 'You got the glory.'

* * *

In a night match at Deal it was panic stations in the Tonbridge dressing room ten minutes before kick-off. We only had seven players.

Harry went and saw the referee and demanded: 'These lights are sub-standard, we can't possibly play'. They went out and stood in the centre circle before the referee said, 'Nonsense, get your team out'.

A minute later Harry was back in the referee's room. 'One goal is smaller than the other, we are not playing.' Out they went again and with the crowd totally bemused Harry and the referee paced out one goal and then went to the other end and paced out the other.

It was eight o'clock before the game started and we just packed our goal and hoped the missing four players arrived. Just before half time, with us 2-0 down, they turned up and we managed to fight back, force extra time and go on and win the game. It was about 10.30 when we got the winner — thanks to Harry.

*   *   *

One of the most embarrassing moments of my life came at a promotion cocktail party for Luton at the Hatters Club. Alec Stock insisted that all the players wear dinner jackets and so I had to go into Dunstable to hire one.

When I went to put the trousers on I discovered that the shop had given me the wrong pair. They would have been too big for a six-foot-six Cyril Smith.

Julie quickly pinned up the bottoms and I found an old pair of braces. I still looked like a clown when I left home and told Julie in the car: 'No dancing, I am not getting up off my chair'.

No sooner had the band started playing than Eric Morecambe came up and said, 'Come on Malcolm, start dancing, you can't keep your wife waiting all night'. I was too embarrassed to explain and just said, 'Sorry, Eric, I can't dance'.

Five minutes later he was back, this time with his wife. He whisked Julie on to the floor and left me with no alternative, I had to dance.

It didn't take the rest of the room long to notice my problem and I think the only person in the Hatters Club who didn't realize was Mrs Morecambe. 'What are they staring at, why has everyone stopped dancing?' she kept asking.

The more I moved, the more my trousers bounced up and down. Out of the corner of my eye I saw Eric holding his sides with laughter.

15

It's tough up front

There is no greater feeling in football than scoring goals. From the days in Bishops Park, Fulham when I shot white plastic Frido balls through sticks to my last goal at Stamford Bridge on 14 May 1979, goals have meant something special to me. Even when I played at full back for Tonbridge and Fulham, I watched enviously as the No. 9 turned to salute the crowd and accept the congratulations of his team-mates.

In my ten years I scored 191 League goals in 369 matches, 28 in the FA Cup and 21 in the League Cup. And I remember every one of them. They all hold special memories. Some were spectacular, some I rate more important and better than others, and some just rolled over the line off my backside. But they all counted, and that is what is important to an out-and-out goalscorer. I have never looked upon myself as anything else. I was not a striker or a forward, I was simply a goalscorer. Roy of the Rovers, my first hero, used to get some great goals in the *Tiger* comic, and then Jimmy Greaves became my idol and I am proud that only Greaves has got a better post-war record than me. He used to bring a smile of pleasure to my face as he popped up in the last minute with the winning goal. The defenders would look at each other in amazement and seem to ask: 'Where did he come from?'

That is exactly what I liked doing. Drop a centre half to his knees in frustration by scoring late in the game. It is the ultimate gesture to someone who has kicked, pushed and hacked at your ankles all afternoon.

When you analyse football it is ironic that thousands of people watch it in the hope of being entertained. They go home happy only if their side has won, and that means the pressure is on the goalscorer. And yet all week one man, perhaps two, have been told how to stop him scoring. It is their job to keep the goalscorer quiet at all costs. They have failed if he escapes from their clutches. Some do their job fairly. Others are animals. You get to know who is going to kick you and you even brace yourself for their first tackle. They want to try and unsettle you, and the first tackle is always the worst: their best effort, something they hope will really frighten you.

I would like to think my reputation with the top defenders in the country was as a dangerous goalscorer and someone who didn't often retaliate. I always preferred to get my own back with a goal rather than a punch.

I broke my golden rule once when I was sent off for hitting Terry Yorath, Coventry's Welsh international who is now at Tottenham, in the opening minutes of a First Division match at Highbury in November 1977. The one thing I couldn't stand was the over-the-top tackle or the sneaky player who came in from behind when the ball had gone. You have got no chance. Those are the tackles that cause the serious injuries.

There is no doubt in my mind that Terry has got the wrong reputation in football and on this occasion the ball was almost at the other end of the field when he came in. Liam Brady had released the ball to Graham Rix when Yorath's tackle came through and for once I just saw red. As I turned, his face was in line with my fist and I hit him once, hard. There were not many people on the ground who saw what happened, but one of them was the referee and I had to go. It was my fault, I was fined by Arsenal, and took full responsibility. I even paid the penalty of missing a return to St James' Park the following week.

The Yorath incident was only the second time I received my marching orders in ten years. I had been sent off previously after a ludicrous incident during an Anglo-Italian Cup tie between Newcastle and Torino at St James' Park. Terry Hibbitt and a tiny Italian winger got into a scrap and I rushed between them to pull them apart. The Italian, who only came up to my chest, then threw a punch at me. I held him at arm's length and shouted at the referee, 'Come on, sort this out'. I couldn't believe it when he sent me off with the little winger and left Hibbitt shrugging his shoulders in apology on the pitch.

Our coach Keith Burkinshaw met me as I trooped slowly off and said: 'What's going on, why are you coming off?' I was so angry: 'That idiot referee has sent me off for trying to stop a fight. It's all that winger's fault.'

My cool burst again and I decided to get my own back on the little pest. I waited by the visitors' dressing room, pinned him up against a wall and hit him three times. As he fell down there was a hand on my shoulder and I just managed to elbow an Italian official as he came up behind me. Down he went. It was getting like something out of *The Sweeney*, and a third Italian was just about to clobber me when another of our party appeared from nowhere and laid him out with a superb right-hander.

We just stood there looking at each other, my colleague in his track suit and me in my kit. The game was still going on and there were three of the Italian party flat out in the players' tunnel.

'You had better go back to the bench', I told him. 'Don't mention it to anyone.' I went and had a bath and waited for the rest of the players to return.

'Have you seen what's out there?' they all asked. 'That little winger and two of his mates are spreadeagled all over the floor.'

I just grinned and said: 'Really? I wonder how that happened.' And that was the last I heard of it.

I am not particularly proud of that story but I hope it demonstrates the kind of pressure players are under. Sometimes you crack and react in the wrong way.

Nor am I pleased with my reaction to being kicked all over the pitch by the Roma centre half in another Anglo-Italian cup tie. Jack Taylor, who was one of the best referees England has produced before he retired in May 1977, was in control and, possibly because he didn't want to appear biased, he was not giving me enough protection.

The defender was handing me out some terrible stick and so I decided to take the law into my own hands. For the only time in my career I went over the top. There was a 50-50 ball and I went for him with no feeling. He was carried off with a smashed knee and I felt no sympathy. He was an animal. Taylor saw what I had done and, technically, should have sent me off. 'I know you have taken some stick but never do that again in your life', he told me as they helped the centre half on to a stretcher. I will never understand why he didn't take action earlier against the Roma player.

To my horror they sent on a man mountain who appeared to be six foot six inches in every direction. He spat at me, kicked me, punched me and hoofed me up in the air every time I touched the ball. It was a frightening experience.

Again I decided to get my own back and although it was probably bravery taking over from sanity I waited for him in the tunnel. I was first player to reach the dressing-room area and I checked our door for a quick getaway. 'Damn', I thought, 'it is locked.' As I was fumbling with the door 'my friend' came up behind me, took my hand and said in broken English: 'Good game, well played'.

We just stood, shaking hands and nodding at each other.

I admit that I went over the top only to prove that forwards can take so much before they snap. They are the men who know that whatever the game, whatever the country and whoever the team, they are going to suffer punishment.

The best thing that happened to forwards was the referees' clampdown in 1971 when the tackle from behind was stamped out. Of course defenders still use it today, but it is illegal in the officials' eyes. There could have been broken legs every week before the charter. The tackles just came through at any height. If you had your back to the goal and the ball was played up to you it was just a question of gritting your teeth and waiting for the worst.

In the Southern League with Tonbridge it was particularly bad. If they had taken the ball off during some matches no-one would have noticed.

Tommy Smith of Liverpool had one of the hardest reputations in football and there was no love lost between Smithy and me. Yet I didn't mind playing against him because you knew what to expect from the moment you ran out. It was a man-against-man challenge.

Norman Hunter of Leeds and Tottenham's Mike England were the same. They were tough characters who never gave an inch and you grew to respect them. It was a battle, one against one and it always ended in the right spirit.

A forward hasn't got a chance if an opponent decides to break the law. It is no contest. Johnny Giles, Leeds' brilliant midfield player, was someone I was never quite sure about. The first time he caught me remains one of the worst tackles I have suffered. Newcastle were playing Leeds and I had just shot over the bar when Giles crashed into me and scythed me across the thighs. You know when it is a bad tackle and a sick feeling spreads from your stomach. It is then you are tempted to retaliate, but something usually holds you back. Giles wasn't punished for his late, ugly challenge although he was, over the years, found guilty by his fellow-professionals. We all respected his ability but were wary of his tackling.

The man I hated playing against the most, and for no physical reasons, was Arsenal's Peter Simpson. I knew I was quicker, more powerful than Simpson but he destroyed me every time. He would drive me mad by talking throughout the game. It was either too wet, too windy or too hot for him. 'I can't run with you today', he would say. 'If you get the right ball you will murder me.' Then he would just get a toe to the ball and knock it out of play or curl his left leg around you and get in a superb tackle.

On his day Simpson was for me as good as Bobby Moore. He didn't have the personality or want the glory, but he was vastly under-rated. If you asked the players to name the most consistent No. 6 in the last ten years, Simpson would run Moore a close second.

There were no rough edges to Simpson, it was all class. The same applied to Roy McFarland at Derby. I played against him a number of times and the only emotions he used were for stirring up his own side. I can't remember one really bad foul from Roy. There was certainly no moaning or dissent. When McFarland and Moore played at the back for England it was a superb partnership. They were two of a kind, ice cool in heated situations, just using their skill to get out of awkward positions.

Forwards can attempt to get the better of defenders in two ways. By scoring, of course, and a verbal attack that your opponent will either rise to or laugh off.

Jack Charlton, the Leeds and England centre half, never liked backchat, as I discovered on our first meeting. I decided to test Jack out and in the opening minute I turned to him and said: 'I used to watch you play years ago, Jack, on the terraces'.

He went berserk galloping after me for the rest of the game. 'I'll get you', he stormed, 'you little upstart.' I was amazed an experienced player like Charlton reacted like that but delighted because it meant I had won. He concentrated on me more than the game and Newcastle beat Leeds that day.

Colin Todd of Derby, who is now at Birmingham via Everton, was one player it was impossible to ruffle. He remained cool at all times. The highlight of our meetings was some tremendous sprinting. We used to have private bets who was going to win over certain distances during the game. Toddy was always hard but fair.

Not like a big bad defender I came across when Luton played

Shrewsbury one season at Kenilworth Road. Alf Wood was their
hard man and his instructions were plain from the first minute:
'Stop Malcolm Macdonald'. We kicked off and set our usual
plan into motion. The ball was played back to Mike Keen, who
sent it through for me. I looked over my shoulder for the pass,
only to be knocked completely off my feet by Wood's challenge.
Wood had apparently hit me across the body with his right arm,
only the referee didn't see it that way. As I picked myself up he
just said: 'Watch where you are going, No. 9, don't run into
defenders'.

Wood's challenge taught me an early lesson. I knew immediately that Shrewsbury looked on me as a danger and that was
the only way they thought they could stop me. From that day I
made up my mind never to allow a centre half the pleasure of
showing I was rattled or injured. I only broke that rule on rare
occasions of extreme provocation.

In fact the more I was kicked, the more I almost liked it. I
knew my opponent was scared of me. Jim Holton, when he was
at Manchester United under Tommy Docherty, just used to go
round the field whacking everyone in sight. I felt sorry for him
during some games as the instructions came out of the dugout:
'Jim, he's the one, get him. Come on Jim, get more tackles in.'

The finest goalkeeper I have played against is undoubtedly
Peter Shilton of Nottingham Forest and England. He has broken
my heart on so many occasions.

It was Shilton, twisting and turning in mid air, who produced
the finest save I have seen from any goalkeeper in the world.
Newcastle were playing at Leicester and I caught a volley
perfectly. A player knows when he has struck the ball well, it
feels right, and on this occasion I watched as it shot towards the
top corner. I was turning in celebration when Shilton just
appeared from nowhere and actually caught the ball one-
handed. The whole of Filbert Street went silent for a split second
as everyone realized they had witnessed something special.

One of the biggest arguments in football during recent years
has been who is the better goalkeeper for England, Shilton or
Ray Clemence. There is no doubt in my mind that Shilton is the
better.

I was always a bit wary of playing against Clemence. He
combines good goalkeeping with a tough approach. He lets you
know that he rules the area, and that means a fist or a boot can
be left 'in' when you challenge him for crosses or rebounds.

Forwards live in constant danger of receiving injuries and knocks, and I'm certain that in the second half of the season players are gambling on fitness to stay in the side. No-one likes to admit he is injured and we would rather carry a niggle than drop out. The greatest healer of any injury is time, but footballers don't get any. Most strains and pulls that players suffer need about ten days' rest, but usually the most a club can afford is three. If you are injured on Saturday and the injury isn't serious, you could be out playing again on Tuesday night.

The pressure on a goalscorer to remain fit is tremendous. I have played when I should have been sitting at home with my leg up simply because I was needed for a crucial match.

I am not talking about playing on when you are in obvious pain, but agreeing to patch up minor injuries because the club needs you. This, however, can eventually cause permanent damage.

I have already mentioned how Arsenal persuaded me to carry on when I knew I needed a cartilage operation at Christmas. I stuck it out, played below my best and regretted it ever since. My advice to anyone is: don't risk playing with injuries, it isn't worth it. There are many players in the First Division today doing permanent damage to themselves because of our club commitments. Unless an injury can actually be seen a player doesn't like to say: 'I don't think I can make it today'. So out he goes and gambles.

We have allowed ourselves to be committed to too many matches in this country. The demand on players is fantastic. It is virtually impossible for one man at the top to sustain peak form over something like 60 matches a season.

But our Football League is still the envy of every other country in the world and, if all players were asked if they would like a mid-season break, a shorter season, or fewer matches, the answer from the majority would be no. They would rather take the risk.

16

Memories

Among the things a man can never lose are his memories. They
are his greatest gifts and, while a display cabinet at my home in
Radwell, Bedfordshire acts as a constant reminder of ten years
in football, my mind holds all the special prizes of my life.

Material things have never meant a lot to me and if Julie had
not packed away my football mementos I certainly wouldn't
have bothered. I lost my three Wembley loser's medals long ago
and have only a few England shirts and caps dotted around the
house. The others have been given away to players to auction off
at their testimonial dinners or handed to schoolboys. The excitement and joy on their faces meant more to me than keeping
them folded away in a drawer.

You will never hear me, either, shouting about what I have
achieved in football. I know what I have done and that is good
enough.

The record book says that Malcolm Macdonald didn't win
much, a few England caps and a hat-trick of loser's medals at
Wembley. That is false. I won more than medals and cups could
give me. It was a long journey from Finlay Street, Fulham to
scoring five goals in one match for England, but I made it. And
along the bumpy way I hope I made a lot of supporters happy
with my goals and gained respect of people I admire in the
game.

I would like to think that I helped a few youngsters just
starting in the game and turned others into better players. I
enjoyed playing alongside and learning from experienced professionals and I tried to do the same for men like Frank Stapleton
of Arsenal.

Football has given me financial security and the chance to
plan my future. It has taken me to different corners of the world
and given me the chance to mix with every walk of life. People

have always fascinated me and I hope that by moving amongst the men in the pub and then VIPs and communicating with them all I have emerged as a better person.

Sport is a universal conversation and football has allowed me to step inside many different worlds and establish a greater understanding and awareness of people and their problems. I can cope with now and tolerate people more than I once could and look back at my past and be self-critical. I appreciate the changes in me, how my bad ways have been corrected and good ways improved.

I have always been a man of principle and I will fight tooth and nail for what I think is right, or what I know is mine. That is why I will always have enemies and upset people.

People represent the biggest challenge in life to me: what makes a man do certain things. I will never understand, for instance, why Don Revie didn't feel responsible enough to sign those goodbye letters to Alan Ball and me. He may have hated us or thought we were two of the worst players in the country, but surely he should have shown us enough respect to put pen to paper? I would have preferred a phone call and if he had made the effort I would have forgiven Don Revie. I would never have forgotten the way he ended my England career but I would have forgiven him for what I consider a dirty trick. Revie took the easy way out. He wasn't man enough to tell the truth.

Gordon Lee and Terry Neill also represent mysteries to me. I don't understand them, how they work, why they make certain decisions. I need to discuss things, take people into my confidence, but I never found it possible with these two men. There was a barrier and I don't fully understand why. Why was it easier for me at Arsenal to speak with Denis Hill Wood, a grand old man, than to someone of my own age, manager Terry Neill, about the same problems?

I continually read biographies of the world's great men to find out more answers. The three people I admire most and whom I would have loved to have met are John F. Kennedy, Winston Churchill and Tito. An evening in their company, to ask them so many questions and to discover what made them tick, would have been so rewarding.

One of the most interesting and satisfying evenings of my life came when I was invited to 10 Downing Street by the then Prime Minister James Callaghan to attend a reception for our paraplegic Olympic team. I spent twenty minutes talking to

Mr Callaghan and he impressed me more in a short space of time than any other man I have met. He was so knowledgeable about every person in that room, bothering to communicate, caring to discuss minor details. If he had told me Arsenal's injury problems at Highbury that day I wouldn't have been surprised. He didn't need to be impressed with me, but the fact that everyone responded to Mr Callaghan is a great compliment to him.

It is impossible not to feel terrific admiration for handicapped people who compete in sport and do things with their lives. I talked that evening with a blind girl of seventeen who had run the 100 metres; suddenly being forced to retire at 29 didn't seem so bad. I was completely naive about the kind of standard these people achieve at athletics, and she staggered me when she said her fastest time at sprinting was just over eleven seconds. My speed has always been one of my greatest assets and the fastest I was clocked over the same distance was 10.7. The world record when this book went to print was 9.9 seconds, which proves the tremendous determination, dedication and courage of these people. The athletes are all timed separately, and the girl explained that to run in a straight line and therefore clock the fastest time her coach stands behind the finishing line blowing a whistle and she just follows the sound.

If I had to pin down the highlights of my playing career they would all revolve around goals. My five against Cyprus, scoring in England's victory over World Champions West Germany, getting a hat-trick for Arsenal in my first game against Newcastle, and of course my Newcastle debut at St James' Park.

Gaining promotion from the Third Division with Luton holds a special place too. We were a family all fighting together. Alec Stock wanted to go up so badly and we did it for him.

The magic and misery of Wembley on Cup Final Saturday is another highlight, despite three Wembley defeats. Wembley will always remain my favourite ground.

My first goal in League football for Fulham against Crystal Palace and the last for Arsenal against Chelsea will always be special memories, and the one I perhaps treasure as much as any of them came at Wembley against West Germany. It was the Germans' first match since they had beaten Holland to win the World Cup in 1974 and we were desperate to beat them. It was only a friendly but the atmosphere was electric, even before we got out on to the pitch. We were urging each other on in the dressing room, we couldn't wait for the game to start. Alan Ball,

Alan Hudson and Colin Bell were magnificent in midfield that
night and Ball combined with Southampton's Mike Channon to
set up the chance for me to head England's second goal.

The best individual goal I ever scored was at St James' Park
against Leicester. Irving Nattrass broke out of defence and
accelerated down the left. Four of us raced through the middle
and any of us could have taken the ball on when his squared pass
flatfooted the Leicester defence. It came to me first and I just hit
it from about 30 yards. Technically I was wrong but it felt good
from the moment it left my left foot and was still going up when
it went into the top corner. Leicester manager Jimmy Bloom-
field tried to blame his goalkeeper afterwards, but every player
knew that Mark Wallington had no chance.

My worst miss came at Blackpool in the League Cup. Arsenal
were playing badly and they were fighting like mad for a shock
result. We desperately needed a goal to settle us down, and a
cross from the right left me only five yards out and with a simple
header. The goalkeeper was stranded and as I turned round
with my arm already in the air to acclaim the goal I completely
missed the ball.

The goals that gave me most satisfaction must be my three
against Newcastle at Highbury. It was my first game against
Newcastle since my transfer and I had mixed feelings of excitement, nerves and apprehension during the morning build-up.
Would Gordon Lee want to talk, how would my old team-mates
react, what reception would the Geordie fans give me now? The
pre-match build-up had been full of predictions, promises and a
few nasty comments from Geoff Nulty, one of Lee's men at
Newcastle. A few of the Newcastle team, the ones I expected to,
came up for a chat before the kick-off, but there was no real
warmth any more. We didn't really have anything in common
now I had left.

It is strange that footballers in the same side really have only
one thing in common: the will to fight and win for your club.
You can live through hundreds of incidents together but with
some in the end you are no closer than when it all began. There
are exceptions of course, but basically teams are just a group of
men with only one real thing in common. Football.

I had no need to worry about my reaction from the Newcastle
fans. They gave me a good reception. It's more than Newcastle
did once the game started and Micky Burns, the man who had
replaced me in the centre of the attack, opened the scoring.

Paddy Howard, also playing against Newcastle for the first time since he left St James' Park, waved his fist at me as Arsenal kicked off again and it worked. Alan Ball chipped over one of his special free kicks and I managed to rise above Alan Kennedy and head it into the opposite corner.

Trevor Ross and Frank Stapleton made it 3-1 by half time and then Stapleton mis-hit a shot straight to me and I couldn't miss to make it 4-1. Everything was going as I dreamed, Newcastle were getting beaten easily and I was scoring goals. It was a good feeling.

Then slowly the tide began to turn and Alan Gowling and Burns again pulled goals back for them. I couldn't believe what was happening. Everyone was shouting at the same time, Newcastle with determination in their voices and us with panic.

The incredible happened however when George Armstrong sent Ross overlapping down the right. Trevor produced a perfect cross to the far post and I managed to get up under pressure and head it down into the net: my hat-trick goal. Highbury went wild with delight and I put one arm up in celebration as the rest of the Arsenal team raced over to congratulate me. Liam Brady tried to force me to rush back in front of the Geordie fans and taunt them. 'Go on Mal, give it to them', he shouted as he tried to lift both my arms above my head. It was not necessary to take it out on the Geordie fans. They had always been good to me. I knew who would be hurt most by my goals.

After the game Gordon Lee was asked the inevitable questions by waiting reporters and his answer was predictable: 'I still say I did the right thing in letting Macdonald go'. I didn't get involved in another slanging match. For the time being my hat-trick had slammed the door shut on Newcastle.

I have never kept records of my goals. Although I remember them all I couldn't tell you how many I got for each of my clubs and I was delighted and proud when I was once told that I am one of only two players who have scored hat-tricks for England, in the Football League, FA Cup and League Cup. The first to do it was West Ham's Geoff Hurst. I am not boasting about that record, but it is a nice feeling when you see it in black and white.

The most embarrassing defeat I have suffered came in an FA Cup replay on 5 February 1972 when non-League Hereford were given no chance against the might of First Division Newcastle. The fact that Hereford had drawn 2-2 at St James' Park was dismissed as a fluke result.

It turned out to be a complete nightmare. We stayed in Hereford for almost a week waiting for their pitch to be declared fit. When we did eventually get started it was like playing on a ploughed field. That suited Hereford, and although I put Newcastle ahead, the home side knocked us out with the help of one of the great goals in Cup history. Ronnie Radford was the scorer and I can still see his 35-yard shot tearing into the top corner. I was standing about ten yards behind Radford when he let go and I remember thinking to myself: 'Don't bother to dive, Willie, that's going in'. You would have thought Hereford had won the Cup as the crowd came on.

They were back again later when Ricky George came on as substitute to score the winner. The television cameras were there and the BBC rubbed salt into Newcastle's wounds for months by playing back the two famous Cup goals of 1972. Radford and George became household names overnight.

I once scored five goals in an FA Cup tie against Nottingham Forest and still finished on the losing side. Luton were drawn away to Nottingham Forest in the 1970 third round and we were all convinced we should have won after an amazing incident. As a Nottingham Forest defender raced back to try and clear a goal-bound shot off the line from me, he crashed into the net and one of the posts snapped at the base. It didn't matter to me as the ball still ended up in the back of the net. Incredibly the referee, after leading us off for twenty minutes while the post was repaired, gave a goal kick.

I scored two and then got a hat-trick in a magnificent replay at Kenilworth Road, but Forest won 4-3.

Memories too are made of things people say and funny incidents that reveal the true character of a person. A manager and coach can talk for hours to their players but one tiny throw-away line can stick in the mind forever.

Martin Peters, who has had a magnificent career with England, West Ham, Spurs and Norwich, remembers one thing that Ron Greenwood said to him when they were together at Upton Park. The players were sitting in the dressing room after a game and Greenwood said to Peters: 'Martin, that half-chance you missed, I bet you would have tucked that away for England'. Peters must have sat through hundreds of team talks and discussions with England's manager but that is the one conversation in detail he can remember. And he doesn't know why.

I discovered Eric Morecambe's character and true sense of humour after an incident many years ago in the Luton dressing room. We had just lost a long unbeaten home record to Gillingham when Eric came into the dressing room: 'Don't worry, lads', he said. 'It is not the end of the world.'

Any dressing room straight after a game is a very private place, especially after a defeat. Frustrations are released, rows started and ended; the last person you want to see is a well-meaning director. Even if it is Eric Morecambe. A boot, thrown from the other side of the room, just missed our famous comedian and as he backed out of the door a chorus of 'Why don't you ... OFF?' sent him on his way. It wasn't a personal insult and anyone would have got the same treatment. We didn't see Eric at Kenilworth Road, however, for about two weeks and a group of the players went to his Harpenden home to see what was the matter.

'No, I can't come back', he said. 'I made a terrible mistake and as a professional I should have realized. The last thing I want to hear after a bad performance on stage is someone saying "It's not the end of the world".'

We eventually persuaded him to return and after our next home game, which we won, there was a polite knock on the dressing-room door. Eric stuck his head inside and shouted at the top of his voice: 'Why don't you ... OFF?', and slammed the door shut.

I also have a fond memory of someone who is now dead, Stan Seymour, the Newcastle director who was loved by everyone at St James' Park. Newcastle were interested in me and Stan was sent to Kenilworth Road on a spying mission. After the game I bumped into him as he was being carried down the stairs by two Luton stewards. Stan was singing his head off. As he passed me he managed to slur: 'Don't worry, Malcolm, old chap, you will be in black and white next season'.

It took me a couple of minutes to realize that Luton and Newcastle wear the same colours.

And then the last memory of my playing career, my last goal against Chelsea. It was nothing special, a far-post header after David O'Leary had broken through and crossed. I didn't realize at the time, of course, that I would never score again but now it holds a place of honour along with my first. The Arsenal crowd, who had always been good to me, gave me a tremendous ovation as I trotted back to the middle. It was almost as if they knew I would never be the same again and I hope they have fond memories of Malcolm Macdonald.

17

The coach is always right

A group of experienced players stand listening to one man in the middle of a field on a cold, wet November morning. He is pointing, explaining, sometimes shouting, always trying to sound interesting. Then for the second time since the group began training the man orders them into a gruelling session of sprinting and exercises. This time he has a stop watch and takes great delight in telling someone he couldn't beat his wife over 50 metres, let alone next Saturday's opposing full back.

The players begin to mock each other; they all want to be the fastest that morning. The slowest man takes unbelievable stick from everyone. It is a game within a game. But it is an important game for it produces spirit and a bond between the group. They are laughing, swearing violently, cursing each other. The man in charge is happy now. He has got them going, it is a good session.

Then at last he produces some footballs and a five-a-side match begins. The players are happy now. They are warm with work and feel like expressing themselves, or if they are unhappy they can take their frustration out on the ball or a team-mate. If a player has lost his place in the side he can now prove to the man in charge that he was wrong. The group are happy playing, shouting. They don't like it when they are told to play two-touch or special marking functions, they just want to play.

The man in charge starts to take stick now as he stops the game to talk some more. The ball is forgotten again as two players are singled out to practise a certain move. 'Come on, that's kids' stuff', they shout and the leader, sensing frustration is growing, throws them the ball again.

If all that sounds boring, then it only goes to prove how vital it is for a coach to make the life of a footballer interesting. It is the easiest thing in the world to get a man fit by driving him on through a continuous slog of running and exercises, but the test of the coach is his ability to express himself and influence his players. And this must be done through the day-by-day routine of training, practice matches, gym work and weights. It is no good talking a good game and being able to organize if the coach doesn't have the ability to make players interested and manipulate his group into a good side. Players are waiting for instructions, they want to learn new things, they want to be directed.

If a number of football supporters were asked who are the best coaches in England they would all say the same: Dave Sexton, Terry Venables, Don Howe ... all the popular choices. They would be right, but they probably wouldn't have a clue why these men are the best. It is because they communicate with players, they have new ideas and they make life interesting. They have the ability to influence a player and then the entire team.

An FA coaching badge doesn't mean that a man is good at his work in the same way as a handful of O and A levels doesn't make a person the best qualified for a certain job. Exam certificates will not suddenly give a journalist flair or a gift for writing.

Good coaches, of course, are not only to be found in the top two divisions. Norwich manager John Bond once said about Gerry Summers, who is now at Gillingham: 'Gerry's teams are always well organized, play attractive football and give you a hard fight. The man should be coaching better players. He is wasted down there in the Third Division.'

There are hundreds of Gerry Summers around but they don't get the recognition. Against that, there are people in the First Division who, I believe, are not good coaches. Gordon Lee's work at Newcastle left me cold and bored; it was an effort to go training every morning, but he has now got one of the best jobs in football as manager of Everton.

The Arsenal players were desperate for someone to communicate with before Don Howe arrived. They were frustrated and unhappy with Terry Neill and that is dangerous. It is rather like a child at school having a teacher he doesn't like or respect. His work suffers and he starts complaining to his parents that he is unhappy. Then a change of teacher lifts the child and he responds. He feels part of the group once more.

Coaches play a very major part in every team's success. They are important to the players and the manager and I can't help feeling that the Continental system is best where a general manager controls contracts, transfers and the financial side of the club, and the coach is left to live with the players. The team is his one responsibility.

At the start of my career I must have been a nightmare to work with. I was unorthodox, stubborn and a problem to fit into any team plan. I just wanted to score goals and refused to listen to advice. Keith Burkinshaw, my first coach at Newcastle, used to tear his hair out in frustration as I turned my back on his help. It wasn't because I didn't respect 'Burky', but I was just obsessed with scoring. If I was getting goals I didn't see any reason to change. Then I listened, learned and, I hope, became a better player.

The first person to influence me was undoubtedly my father. He loved football and it rubbed off on me. Then as I watched more Fulham games I became interested in Johnny Haynes and the impact he had on an entire match. Bobby Smith of Tottenham was the next, I admired his courage, the way he barged defenders out of the way to score goals and after that I always wanted to be the big centre forward in kick-about matches at the local park. If I wasn't playing well I switched to someone else. One day I was Haynes making goals and the next I would turn into Smith and score some.

Sports masters at school took over from idols, although my father always kept an eye on my development. He once told me: 'Don't take any notice of the man at school, son, he hasn't got a clue. Do it my way. Go and watch the professionals.'

Then part-time and amateur coaches worked with me before I moved through the First Division to arrive and end with the best I have played under, Don Howe. Howe is superb at organizing teams and as a former full back he worked particularly brilliantly with Arsenal's defence. He therefore has done more for someone like Willie Young than myself because he understands Willie's problems.

Players are always looking for something new, and Alan Ball senior impressed me one day during training in Sweden. He was coaching Djurgaarden when he suddenly blew a whistle to stop a practice match and put his hands over the eyes of the nearest player. He then asked the player to point out and describe exactly where the members of his own team and the opposition were standing. It was an exercise in awareness and the player was disappointed when he failed to locate more than one. My team-mate was shattered because all week the coach is the most important man in the players' lives. They are trying to impress him. They either want to stay in the side or get back in and he is the man who will influence selection.

Once a team leaves the dressing room on match days and leaves the coach behind, there is not much more he can do to help their performance. He can shout instructions, alter positions but it is basically up to the players to put his weeks' work into practice. He always becomes important in a crisis, however. If a player is sent off, the others always look to the coach to sort it out. They don't want to take the responsibility of changing tactics or moving the team around. If something goes wrong in the game and it is lost the players can blame the coach.

The coach is also the most important man on the ground at half time. That is his period, he can see what is going wrong and the players always show him their respect of letting him talk and listening. If he wants to change the tactics, substitute a player, move others around, it is done at half time.

At Arsenal the captain is encouraged to join in any discussion. After the coach has finished talking the captain is asked if he has anything to add. It is a show of respect. The senior players, in turn, too are called on to make observations; often at Highbury a referee was kept waiting to start the second half while we all tried to solve any problems.

That is good. Players like to be involved, they want to be asked. A situation should never develop when a player feels on the outside of things. To be dropped and stuck in the reserves is bad enough for an experienced player, to be in the first team and frozen out is worse.

I have never thought that captains have a great influence on other players during a game. The theory that a captain is an extension of his manager is a myth. A captain can encourage and help the young inexperienced player and represent the team when any crisis arises on and off the field, but he can't dictate how a team plays.

Alan Ball is perhaps one exception I have played under. He used to run team meetings at Highbury before Don Howe arrived and influenced a lot of players at Arsenal before he left for Southampton.

Bobby Moncur at Newcastle was a better captain than player. He demanded 100 per cent from everyone with his own character and will to do well. He led by example. The crowd responded to him and that, too, is important for a skipper.

All coaches are different of course, but there is one annoying tactic they all have in common and that is sending big central defenders up into attack for the last fifteen minutes when the game is slipping away.

I have never understood what purpose the arrival of an extra man achieves. I can just about understand them being sent up for corners and free kicks, but not to play as a third centre forward. Newcastle used to do it a lot with my old friend Paddy Howard, and after one particular game my strike partner John Tudor and I argued with Keith Burkinshaw: 'What good does it do? He is only taking up space that is valuable to us.'

Defenders sent racing into forward positions seem to take it as a personal insult if they don't get a touch to corners or free kicks. And when they stay up for longer periods the rest of the forward line doesn't have a clue what is going on.

Willie Young at Arsenal is always used as an emergency battering ram, and Luton sent Terry Branston forward in every emergency. In one match Graham French and Matt Tees produced a superb move to create a chance for me and I was just about to head the ball into an empty net when Branston crashed into me and both of us and the ball ended up in the crowd.

Goalscoring should be left to the experts. A pair of strikers know one another inside out, they know each other's weaknesses and strengths, and the last thing they need is an intruder upsetting plans and carefully worked-out moves.

John Tudor and I were a good team at Newcastle and once against Southampton he made a goal for me without touching the ball, simply because he knew my strengths. A through ball seemed out of reach and we had both slowed down when Tudor shouted: 'Don't stop, you can get that'. I raced on and just pipped goalkeeper Eric Martin to the ball. I had given up any hope of scoring, but John judged that my speed would grab Newcastle a goal.

I always thought that John Radford and Ray Kennedy, when they were together at Arsenal, had that kind of understanding. I rate them as the best forward partnership that I have seen. They seemed to hit it off without trying, finding each other under pressure and never flinching when the going got tough. They had tremendous respect throughout the First Division and defenders never enjoyed playing against them. Neither man was particularly quick but their positional sense, understanding and bravery were superb.

I have always relied on my speed to carry me into scoring positions and don't believe a coach can do as much for forwards as he can for other players in midfield and defensive positions.

A forward arrives in the area perhaps between twenty and 50 times in a match, but there is only a limited number of ways he can be fed. A coach can devise new plans and different set pieces in an effort to open up the opposition, but the move ends with the ball being played into the danger area at the *same* height or angle. It is up to the forward to get on the end of it.

Most spectacular goals come from outside the area and this is why they are scored more by midfield players or forwards supporting the two front men. It is natural; the forward might take a defender out of position with his run and a gap opens up for a support player to score from 25 yards.

I was once praised for a spectacular goal I scored against Leeds when I received the ball with my back to goal on the edge of the area, turned quickly and drove it into the top corner. It looked good but it was a coach's nightmare. I had my back to Gordon McQueen when I received the ball and turned quickly to my right before shooting. Now Leeds and every other club knew that my left foot was my stronger and McQueen would have been told a number of times during the week: 'Don't let Macdonald turn to his right'. But he faltered once and paid the penalty.

Once a coach has got his players fit he introduces a number of rules — apart from the daily training schedule — to keep their bodies in perfect condition.

Every player likes to feel good and it is ridiculous to start telling grown men not to drink too much and never have sex on a Friday before the game. These are old-fashioned wives' tales. I enjoyed a few pints during the week but was always sensible enough to stop two days before the weekend. I laughed off the no-sex-please argument when Julie and I broke the golden rule one Friday night and on a Kenilworth Road mudheap the next day I scored the first hat-trick of my career against Bradford City!

Most players know how to stay fit and it is only the misguided few who abuse the rules and allow their social life to affect their performance.

Never believe either that players need persuading to compete in too many matches. Playing is better than training and Don Howe encourages players over 26 years old to have only two weeks a year of non-exercise. At that age your fitness level is going down and Howe believes your body needs to tick over. It is no good having a long summer break at 30 with too much rich food and drink and then throwing yourself back into tough pre-season training.

Howe is always introducing new ideas and training schedules, and it is difficult to imagine how much fitter footballers can become or how advanced world coaching can develop.

The change just in my ten years has been staggering and it makes me laugh when people compare yesterday's greats with today's teams. Sir Stanley Matthews was a great player in his era but I doubt if he would be so effective in the First Division now. He wouldn't be able to beat his full back, dribble to the line and cross. He would be closed down, space would be denied him from the moment he got the ball. Players today are far more aware of every aspect of the game; it is a contest of chess with no-one daring to make the wrong move.

But it is a magnificent game and the coaches shoulder the responsibility of keeping it interesting for the players and entertaining for the public.

18

Read the small print

If the Football League and Football Association allowed me two wishes for my retirement I wouldn't have to think twice before making life better for players in this country. I would cancel all footballers' contracts and re-write them, and abolish the disciplinary system as it stands. Both give the players no chance. Both are a joke.

Contracts tie a player's hands behind him and send him out to play on a Saturday afternoon. To go before a Football Association disciplinary committee is like sitting in front of a bogus jury. You haven't got any legal rights.

From the day I was thrown into running our shop in Sussex with my mother I have had to deal with legal documents, and the way players are treated — or let themselves be treated — in this country has always disgusted me. When a player signs on the dotted line he is trapped. The only thing he can re-negotiate is money. The rest of the small print makes up hard-and-fast rules.

A player, like all employees, is paid through PAYE. He is heavily taxed although, of course, he can charge the normal things against his earnings. A footballer will earn more than Mr Average, but don't forget his earning capacity at that level is short. Our pensions begin at 35 years old.

I would like to see every player in this country self-employed and able to hire his services out to the football club of his choice. Then, like a builder or any self-employed person, he could claim the extra tax benefits. At the moment a footballer pays more tax than most as his salary is higher, but the punishment doesn't fit the crime because he is only at that salary level for perhaps ten years of his career.

I made numerous inquiries into this when I was playing and discovered that the main stumbling block was that the FA have not got the legal right to suspend a self-employed person. It would have meant devising a new — and better — disciplinary system, but making revolutionary changes like this in our game is like asking the Queen to play for Crystal Palace ladies team.

I'm sure there is no other group of people except footballers who would stand for the things they are denied in contracts. The wording is the same on them all and I would love to meet the men who first dreamt up clause five. It states: 'A player shall not engage in any business or live in any place which the director of the club may deem unsuitable'.

Now I'm not saying I ever wanted to live on a barge or run a brothel, but surely I should have the right to open a business if it doesn't affect my work with the football club. Many times in my experience a player has fallen out with a manager who has recommended to the Board that a request to open a pub, boutique or small business be turned down. That kind of thing could only happen in football.

All the clauses seem to be one-sided. Like this: 'Under no circumstances shall the player make payment to agents or persons, other than clubs and persons regularly employed by the clubs, and concerned in the engagement of players, with a view to obtaining employment'.

Are they really telling me I can't choose someone to look after my own interests? I have ignored this at all times and if any of my clubs had tried to stop it I would have fought them.

Footballers are always treated like wooden soldiers, people who can't look after themselves. There is, of course, a tiny minority who need careful handling, but the majority want to plan for the future and they want to do it their way.

How on earth can a teenager just coming into the game negotiate properly when he sits down with the manager of the club to discuss his first contract? A first contract always has a bearing on the last and it is the most important day of a player's life. The manager might be a hero to the kid and all that happens is he takes one look at the money and signs. He doesn't read the small print, he just joins the rat race. He should have a solicitor, an accountant or an experienced business man in there with him, explaining just what he is letting himself in for.

I wish players could negotiate their own contracts, re-write clauses, change rules. In football you don't get a choice. The rules are the same for everyone. And if you don't sign you don't play.

Freedom of speech is another game footballers are not

allowed to play. You can say anything, as long as it suits your club. Clause 13, part C takes care of that. It says: 'The player agrees that he will not without permission of club grant interviews to, nor write articles for, newspapers or other publications, nor take part in TV or radio programmes and that he will submit articles etc. to the club for approval before allowing publication'.

What they are saying is that Terry Neill can call his Arsenal players 'morons', but we are not allowed to prove we are not without his permission.

When I was in the North East, Sunderland lost a game at Bristol City and Dennis Tueart read the next morning that he had been slagged off by manager Bob Stokoe. Tueart, apparently, had not even spoken to his manager after the game but he was not allowed to say that. If he had gone to the newspaper and replied he would probably have been suspended or fined. Surely this is outside the law? A man must have the freedom of speech and the right to reply.

After Alan Hudson and I had been sent home from Australia we made up our minds to remain silent about the entire affair. But Terry Neill made certain accusations when he arrived at Heathrow Airport and it was impossible not to be allowed to defend ourselves. I requested special permission from chairman Denis Hill Wood and he accepted that it was my right to give my side of the story publicly.

It is amazing how many players in this country don't even have an accountant. There are men earning in the region of £300 a week and filling in legal documents who don't have a clue about what is happening to them. I once asked a team-mate if he had a solicitor or an accountant and he replied 'No, it's not worth it, I just get my next-door neighbour to give me a hand'. That was an international at the top of his profession.

Players do amazing things that could land them in terrible legal trouble. They sign a contract with a boot company and just black out the white lines on their existing boots. Then, when a third company offers them more money, they sign another contract and end up with three different pairs of boots they are legally supposed to be wearing for League and Cup matches. Again, no guidance.

The story is the same at disciplinary hearings. You are marched into a room, sat down in front of a panel of five men who may hate your guts, and put on trial. I have been to about four of these hearings and they were all a farce. Anyone who actually knows his rights and argues is frowned upon as a troublemaker.

You are not allowed to take a solicitor in with you, but you can either represent yourself or allow an official of the club to talk for you. If you decide to take your manager along to a personal hearing you are not allowed to say a word without the permission of the committee's chairman. If there is no-one at the club you want to defend you, tough luck.

I was once hauled before a disciplinary hearing after someone in the Norwich crowd wrote to the Football Association and complained that I had made a rude gesture towards a linesman. Instead of the FA writing back to their informant and saying they would deal with the matter and then writing to Arsenal asking them to have a word with me, it became a long involved legal tangle. The linesman and referee were asked to supply comments and before I knew what had happened I was charged with bringing the game into disrepute. They had no real evidence, but I was being charged. I was in danger of receiving a two-month ban just because a punter at Carrow Road said he saw me make a gesture.

I give details of what happened next because it only emphasizes what a disgrace these hearings are. Again, it could happen only in football. I wanted to speak for myself but Arsenal secretary Ken Friar explained that it was the club's policy to defend their players and Terry Neill got the job of my counsel. I recall that Vernon Stokes chaired the panel and Bert Millichip, Peter Swales and two regional members of the FA sat with him. I had no complaints about that. I had nothing against any of them.

What actually happened in the Norwich match was that I had a go at a linesman after a bad tackle from their centre half had almost put one of our young players in the stand, but there was no gesture. The referee raced over and I told him: 'A young lad up front with me is getting kicked to bits and there is absolutely no protection from that linesman'. The referee said he would look after it and added: 'You have been booked already, so let's have no more trouble'. The referee confirmed my story at the hearing and I was disappointed that he didn't end the case by adding: 'Gentlemen, I saw the incident and took what action I thought necessary. If I had seen any gesture I would have sent Macdonald off.'

Instead we went into the world of fantasy. Written evidence from the other linesman was read out and, despite being about 80 yards away and me having my back turned to him, he thought he saw my hand move. It was all up to the linesman in question then and he got up and said: 'I have watched television evidence of the incident and my suspicions were confirmed, Macdonald did appear to make a gesture towards me'.

The evidence against me piled up and Terry Neill became my only chance of justice being done. Stokes asked him if he was producing the film for evidence.

'No', said Terry. 'It is not available.'

Stokes then asked Terry if he had seen the TV re-run of the incident.

'Yes', said Terry.

'What is your view?' Stokes added.

I sat in the corner thinking: 'Go on, Terry, you can clear me now, just say there was no gesture. Just tell them the truth.' Instead he produced this classic that sent my stomach sinking to my shoes: 'Well, I don't think it makes the player innocent and I don't think it makes him guilty either'.

It was time to intercept before I ended up in jail, and I asked Stokes 'Can I say something?' There was almost a smile on his face when he replied 'I think you'd better'.

I began to conduct my own defence and asked the linesman where my hand was alleged to have been while I made the gesture. 'By your navel', he answered.

'That's funny', I replied. 'The other linesman said he saw me make a gesture and my back was turned to him. So surely for him to see, my hand must have been either in the air or to the side.'

The linesman looked confused. In fact, I think we all were. 'I don't know about that', he mumbled.

The confusion caused a postponement while television evidence was found and at a later hearing I was found guilty, even though my TV appearance lasted less than two seconds. My punishment was £100 and I suppose I was lucky. It could have been two months. Some clubs pay their players' fines but Arsenal deducted the money from my next wage slip. It is a matter of principle with Arsenal that when a player gets into trouble he pays his own fine, and I agree with them.

Another time I was fined £150 after being sent off for hitting Terry Yorath and thought I got away lightly, especially as Terry Neill had just fined two players £100 for turning up late for training. I deserved to lose a week's wages for being sent off for hitting an opponent.

At another hearing when I appealed against a booking I received for shoulder-charging Chelsea goalkeeper Peter Bonetti, the evidence got just as twisted. I knew the cross had come from the right when I charged Bonetti, but the referee and linesman insisted it was from a left wing centre. They then proceeded to show the committee which way Bonetti had turned and only proved that the cross had come from the right. It didn't really matter because no one took any notice and once again I lost.

The next morning in the Newcastle dressing room I asked the boys who crossed the ball when I was penalized for fouling Bonetti.

'I did', said Stuart Barrowclough. 'From the right.'

These things would never happen if the player was allowed to be represented by a professional. A barrister or solicitor would not allow half of the things that go on behind the locked doors of a disciplinary hearing.

The word in football is always to go before the commission in the morning, as some of the elder councillors get a bit drowsy after a heavy lunch and a few brandies. I appealed against a booking at Coventry once and one of the committee actually fell asleep. He was snoring and had to be nudged back to life to give his verdict of 'guilty'.

The other tip is always try and get local people on your commission because, if the committee have come a long way and the travelling expenses are high, your fine will go up accordingly. There is no way I can prove these, but they are little things that put doubt in your mind.

Personalities also play a big part and Newcastle manager Joe Harvey escorted Frank Clark to a hearing where Clark was appealing against a booking. Joe took one look at the panel, saw Vernon Stokes and said: 'Come on, Frank, we are going. Plead guilty and the club will pay your fine. But I am not staying in this room with that man.' For some reason Joe didn't like Stokes and the last thing he thought of was whether Clark was guilty or innocent.

There are also flaws in the disciplinary points system when, after collecting twenty points, the player is automatically suspended. A player can be booked three times and land on sixteen points but then knuckle down, change his attitude and keep out of trouble for the next three months. Then a referee makes a mistake, books the wrong man and the player ends up banned and disillusioned.

There is also a terrible language problem throughout football. Too many men in power have no understanding of players. Most referees certainly don't, some managers struggle to understand a player's problems, and the men who sit on disciplinary committee are just not on the same wavelength.

Why can't the FA employ a professional barrister for different areas and allow him to sit as the ruling judge at all commissions? It would stop all arguments and injustices and the players would be happy to accept any decision reached. I am not asking for players to be found not guilty. All I want is a fair trial. At the moment it is far from that.

The players are the most important people in football. Without them there would be no sport. Most of their attitudes are the same. They are happy being paid for something they love doing. I just hate to be exploited and used, and believe me, that is how players are treated in this country. And deep down I fear it will never change.

19

Are you really SuperMac?

The stranger at the bar saw me over the top of his beer glass and as soon as our eyes met I knew my quiet night out with Julie was over. 'Hey, there's SuperMac', his voice boomed around the room. I tried not to notice but the first intruder had already stuck a beer mat under my nose to autograph. Julie was just an onlooker now as they fired questions and moved in closer.

That incident in a Newcastle pub is typical of anyone in the public eye and I don't relate it as a criticism of the well-meaning people who like to be seen with the stars. It is just to emphasize a way of life that has turned me into something of a Jekyll and Hyde. The glamour of being recognized and the benefits that go with it are obviously a part of life that I appreciate. I just wish that sometimes I could become plain Malcolm Macdonald and enjoy privacy when my family and I need it.

The social side of our life changed the moment I scored a hat-trick on my Newcastle debut against Liverpool at St James' Park. The Geordies adopted me from that moment as 'SuperMac' and the nickname has stuck ever since. People forgot I was Malcolm Macdonald, they wanted to know SuperMac instead.

While I recognize that SuperMac has been good for me, and in the beginning I loved it, I have since found it a name difficult to live up to. There have been many times when I have just not felt like being him. It is a name that conjures up different pictures in supporters' eyes, and I recall one man being very indignant and saying: 'You're not very big for a SuperMac, are you sure you're the real one?'

For me SuperMac came alive once I ran out at St James' Park in front of the Geordies. I felt like a hero then and wanted to live up to their expectations; after all, Newcastle and their magnificent supporters made me what I am today. I suppose, therefore, I couldn't expect them to change once the game had ended. We had a special relationship and I was their adopted son. In the end it was impossible to go into pubs and clubs and it became very difficult for Julie to tolerate. The Geordies are a marvellous race. Having a few beers and a good time only just knock football into third place in their list of priorities, and a night out with a Newcastle player is their idea of heaven.

Southern supporters are completely different. They haven't the passion and pride of a Geordie. They will come up and ask for an autograph, chat for a couple of minutes and then disappear, not bring you over a pint, sit on your wife's lap and expect to be entertained until the pubs close. That is why I am happy living now in the sleepy Bedfordshire village of Radwell. The pace is slow and the people are not demanding. It is an ideal home for me to start building a new career. For basically, I am a private person. That probably sounds strange from someone who has always been in the headlines and involved in controversial incidents, but I am a man of principle and if anything is worth fighting for, I fight. The rest of the time I am happy to take a back seat.

There are not many people who know me really well, few men whom I would call close. I know whether I like someone instantly and if I want a relationship to grow. My wife is my best friend, she understands me and has taught me a lot. If I have got problems to discuss I go to Julie. She tells me if I am right or wrong or if I have said too much. And her judgement is usually good.

There is a barrier I put up and I suppose that there are two sides of Malcolm Macdonald, private and public.

The only time I really get upset about my nickname is when it affects Julie or my four daughters, Claire Juliette, Jeanette, Louise Elaine and Emily Jane. Once two of the girls were being pestered by a group of boys at school. 'Is your dad really Super-Mac?' they all asked in the playground. 'No he isn't, actually his name is Malcolm Macdonald', Claire, my eldest daughter, said with her nose in the air.

Public image is very important to maintain; one argument with a supporter, one incident of refusing to sign a child's autograph book because you are in a hurry, and your character is blacked for the rest of your career.

It is a tremendous pressure to live under and I had to bite my tongue once on a return train journey after Newcastle had beaten West Ham at Upton Park. The Newcastle fans were obviously in jubilant mood after our victory and a group of them opened our compartment door to ask for some autographs. I was sitting nearest to the door and as one fan leaned across me to ask John Tudor to sign he burned a hole in my trousers with his cigarette. The guy didn't notice, and although I wanted to scream and shout I realized just in time it would have been the worst thing to do. The fan had cost me my win bonus but his image of me would have been ruined if I had let my public face slip.

Although the Newcastle fans treated me like a king I almost missed an important evening game against Leeds because a burly police officer refused to accept that I was Malcolm Macdonald. The main car park at St James' Park is for permit holders only, but the Newcastle players never bothered even to collect their passes. On this night there had been a bomb scare and as I drove through the gate the bobby stood in front of the car. 'If you haven't got a pass you can't come in', he said, waving other cars through.

'Don't be silly, I'm not going to blow the place up, I'm playing', I pleaded.

It was 6.30 p.m. and 40 minutes later I was still there. I signed autographs, talked to supporters, waved to officials, watched as team-mates without passes drove by. But he wouldn't budge and it took the local chief inspector to finally convince his PC that I was telling the truth. You can imagine the reception I got in the dressing room. Keith Burkinshaw was furious and ready to fine me while the players greeted me with the obvious comments. 'We thought you were known around here', they said. 'Call yourself a star — you had better score a few more goals.'

It is amazing what some supporters will do to meet their heroes, without any consideration for what you are doing or who you are talking to. All these incidents happened at Newcastle because in the North East you are accepted as being part of the same big happy family. If a fan sees you in the street he stops and talks to you, he doesn't stare and point to his partner and whisper, he grabs hold of your arm and begins a conversation. If I was sitting down in a restaurant or buying something in a shop in Newcastle, that would be an open invitation for a group of complete strangers to gather round. It is flattering of course, but I would have preferred it if they had waited for a better time and place.

I have never refused an autograph or a chat with anyone, but the pressure of keeping cool in public is tremendous. I just don't know how VIPs and superstars live under a 24-hour spotlight.

I have never been quite sure what to say to the fan who uses a decoy to meet his hero; the man who wheels his two-year-old son up and says: 'He is your biggest fan, can he have your autograph?' You look down and the poor little chap is half asleep and hasn't a clue what is going on or who I am. Why didn't his father just say: 'Hello Malcolm, I have always wanted to meet you'?

Another fella once dragged his girl friend up to me as I stood with some friends and said: 'She has always wanted to meet you, can she have your autograph?' When I asked him for his book he just said: 'No, sign here' and pulled the front of the girl's dress down to her navel. The poor girl, who had been a shade of pink with shyness, turned a bright red and I just walked away out of pity for her. I have never understood what made that man do it. Perhaps he was more embarrassed than any of us.

The public must remain, however, always right, and answering letters and special requests from supporters is another part of a player's life. I send back hundreds of photographs and autographs; I think it is important for fans to receive a personal reply whenever it is possible.

One letter I received, however, dropped me into the middle of a Newcastle police investigation. The letter arrived at St James' Park one morning, full of juicy suggestions, and I didn't think anything of it until I noticed it was signed by a man. We all had a good laugh about it until, for the next three weeks, I received more descriptive prose from the same man. I just threw them away and dismissed the fella as a crank. The content got worse with every letter. Then one morning he wrote that he was the killer of a little lad who had been murdered recently in Newcastle. 'Crank or no crank, you have got to go to the police now', the club told me.

The police insisted that somehow I arrange a meeting with the author, and at the end of a column I wrote for the local newspaper I asked the man who had been writing to me each week to meet me at a certain rendezvous the following day. The police were waiting for him and discovered that my sick friend had been living with the man who had, in fact, murdered the small boy. I still find that story rather sad, and although justice was done it does emphasize the kind of situations a footballer can find himself thrown into. He had obviously just picked on me as someone to write to. I was his shoulder to cry on. He identified himself with me for no reason other than that I was a public figure in Newcastle.

The pressures, sometimes self-inflicted, on a player can become so great that often the only privacy he can enjoy is on the field during a game. That may sound crazy, but at least on the pitch you are out of bounds to anyone except the opposition. You can forget your outside problems and lose yourself in the game. I'm sure someone like Stan Bowles, who has had more pressure to live with than most, has often looked forward to Saturday afternoon as an escape.

Pressure and success are, of course, linked. Players can be thrown overnight into the public eye through television, radio and newspapers.

I believe it was Southampton manager Lawrie McMenemy who said that football managers and players are the only untrained people who have to stand up and give a good account of themselves in public. We were never taught how to keep an audience interested or hold our own under fire from a trained interviewer under the glare of television lights, but it is expected of us. Too many players are dismissed by the public as thick or boring after one brief nerve-racking appearance in public.

Footballers are too often misjudged and I suppose that is why I have always tried to give a good account of myself in front of supporters and the media. I admit that I have often found the pressure difficult to handle, but I have never backed away. Since retiring I have done a lot of radio work and have grown to enjoy it. It can give a tremendous boost to your confidence, which is what half of the players in this country lack when it comes to public speaking.

I hope the image the public have of me has helped the reputations of footballers in this country. I am not an angel, as I have said before, but I have always tried to be honest with supporters and with what I say.

I have lived with a certain amount of pressure in ten years but I wouldn't change much if I could turn back the clock. The setbacks, the rows, the glory, the men I have played under and with, and finally having to quit at 29, have all helped me become, I hope, a better person.

There is no other sport like football for either making or breaking a man.

20

The future

The next ten years are going to be the most important for football that this country has ever known. Our game, respected throughout the world and the most popular sport in this country, will either die or rise again in the next decade. It is up to the men in power, at the Football Association, the Football League and the club chairmen, to save it. If they haven't got any ambition left or stomach to gamble, they should get out and pass over the running of the game to men that care.

I have spent the last ten years of my life as a player and experienced many changes. We have now reached the crossroads and if we are led down the wrong turning by the wrong people there may be no turning back.

While England manager Ron Greenwood is leading a fabulous revival on the pitch, the image of football in England is not good. Idiot hooligans who call themselves supporters have driven true fans away and families are looking elsewhere for their entertainment.

Football is big show business and yet we don't do enough to attract the fans back. We are also selling the game short, running it like a bunch of amateurs instead of demanding the right price for what is still the biggest-selling form of entertainment that this country produces. We have allowed other countries to take our game and overtake us. They are light years ahead of us now in terms of selling the sport, and still we do little about it.

Clubs can help, and the first thing I would like to see is a public relations officer installed at every ground. He or she would be responsible for selling the club and its players to the public through television, newspapers, radio and other commercial avenues. It is crazy for a manager to be 'not available' when he is needed by the Press to comment on a transfer, or a player to be 'gagged' because he might be fined for saying something wrong. Who cares if it is wrong, it's publicity for the club.

Liam Brady is a classic example of how a player should not be treated. Brady is one of the outstanding talents in Europe and yet he remains a mystery. His public image is nil. Arsenal should be shot for not exploiting Brady's talents. When you have got the best, use it. Brady should have been sold to the public as the outstanding midfield footballer in Britain. There should be no question of him refusing, for it would have earned him a lot of money and helped Arsenal pull in more supporters.

Joe Harvey at Newcastle had the right idea. He knew the most important people to his football club were the public. Without them Joe and Newcastle were dead, and that was Harvey's attitude. If a fan was standing on the doorstep when Joe arrived for work, he was invited inside St James' Park. There was none of this: 'You stand out in the cold, and perhaps so-and-so will talk to you after training'.

It may increase the pressure on players, but in the end everyone benefits. I have only learned this by being involved with different clubs during my career. At the beginning I was as green as anyone and happy just to sit back and play; but to sell football is so obviously the right way to operate. It makes me sick when I see clubs just walking along the survival road. They should get up and start running. All the men in power in our game have been around long enough to know that football can't survive as it is at the moment.

The first thing we must do is improve our grounds, make them hooligan-proof and turn shabby old-fashioned stadiums into sports arenas for the entire family. When football first began looking for potential customers in the latter part of the last century it was decided to take the sport to the masses. It was a game for the working class to watch, and because they could not afford to travel the grounds were planted on their doorsteps. Compact little grounds, surrounded by terraced houses and streets, popped up everywhere. Today everyone drives cars, everyone can afford to travel and the emergence of New Town developments means that people are moving away from their original habitat. But the football stadiums remain squashed into tiny spaces.

There has been a population boom and yet football clubs are struggling against falling attendances. Why? Football has a great deal more to compete with, but it is still the most popular sport in the world. The main problem is that we are selling the game of tomorrow surrounded by the amenities and men of yesteryear.

When football began, we gave the supporters what they wanted. It is all about supply and demand. At the moment we are not giving the people what they need. People's demands today are greater in every walk of life and the football fan wants more for his money. He doesn't want to stand in the rain and get sworn at and beaten up by a hooligan. He doesn't want to queue for ten minutes to go to the toilet or have a cup of tea slopped over him. He wants comfort, a place to park his car, a seat at the ground for all his family and other facilities.

If a terrace fan today decides to watch an important game, he has to get to the ground at least two hours before the kick-off and stand around to have any chance of even seeing the action. What a waste of time! There should be facilities for him to have a drink and a meal.

We have been so slow in realizing that we must change. Clubs therefore have got to either extend and enlarge their own grounds or, if that is not possible, move to new sites. Teams close together in one area should combine and share new stadiums that can provide facilities for the future. Nottingham Forest and Notts County, Liverpool and Everton — it doesn't matter how big they are — the fan must come first now. Turn old stands into new ones, put a bowling alley underneath, open up the bars and restaurants every day of the week. If it's possible, do it.

I can hear the laughter and comment of 'We can't afford it' as people read my ideas. The reality is that we have *got* to afford it and, if the directors are not willing to move into the future, then they should allow professional business men into football to start running the game properly. The director who scoffs at these ideas means nothing to football in this country any more. He is just surviving along with the other dead wood. He is treating being a director of a football club as a hobby rather than a business. It is a little bit of prestige for him.

We need sports complexes shared by football clubs and other organizations. Make them all-seater and put up the prices. That would drive the hooligans away. How do you have a riot when the person you want to smash over the head with a bottle is sitting twenty rows away?

It is amazing how the clubs let themselves be undersold. Football is top entertainment and yet only in England would we

charge the same admission for the top of the First Division and
the bottom of the Fourth. That is nothing against the Fourth
Division but, if people want to see the best, they should be
charged more. The man who stands on the terraces at Liverpool
would not expect to pay the same price for a ticket to a Frank
Sinatra concert as he would to go to the circus. So why football?
At every aspect we are selling the game for nothing.

Clubs who have recently built new grandstands at their
grounds should be ashamed of themselves if they have not
included other forms of entertainment and comfort in their
project. There is no excuse for neglecting the supporter any
longer.

I always hear the same old excuses for not wanting to share
stadiums: who plays at home on Saturday, what happens when
we are both drawn at home in the Cup? All I can say is that if we
think those are problems we really have got trouble with the
future of football in this country. Neither am I against a mid-
season break to allow pitches to recover and to prevent the fan
watching in freezing cold conditions. If it seems a good idea then
try it, even experiment one year with summer soccer. You will
never find out if you don't gamble.

Covering of pitches is also an excellent way to prevent a
terrible backlog of fixtures. It is not entertainment when players
have to perform on mudheaps or skate about on ice. Why more
clubs have not followed Leicester's example of covering their
pitch with a balloon I will never know.

I am not saying that all clubs should up and move to a new
home. But, if your ground has not got the space to cater for what
the public now demands, search for a bigger site and, if that
means combining with another club and sharing the cost, why
not? It is not a financial gamble because the missing millions are
waiting to return if the atmosphere is right and the facilities
improved. If we stand still now we are dead. The danger light is
flashing. At the moment it is only a warning ... but tomorrow
may be too late.

Clubs should sell themselves more, and the League and the
FA must increase their promotion of the game. If a shop has got
the best fur coat in the world it puts it on show in the window and
you expect to pay. At the moment football is tied up in a box and
thrown at the back of the shop.

It is not only spectators who are disappearing, but our best
players are beginning to drain to the Continent. How we allowed

that to happen in front of our noses I will never know. We spend
so many hours moaning about minor details and fighting each
other when major issues are left untouched. We seem to concede
defeat to Europe in every aspect of the game. Let's stand up and
fight them for a change. Players are like the public. They want
the best, and if we can't provide it for them they will go elsewhere.

I have become commercial executive at Fulham Football
Club and I am prepared to roll up my sleeves and have a go for
the future of football in England. I know men who share my
view, but I am not sure if they are ever going to be able to make
the big decisions.

It is impossible not to spend ten years as a player and have a
deep feeling for the game. I care for the future and am
desperately keen to put something back into a sport that has
given me a good living.

I am not ready to become a manager because I lack experience and don't believe I could gain the respect yet of players the
same age and older than me. I need administration experience
before taking the giant step into management. If one day I did
take over a club I would do all I could to put my ideas into
practice. I believe it only needs one man, one club to change the
outlook of football for an entire new era to open up.

In 1968 when I signed for my own local club Fulham I was
excited about the future of the game. And I was right because it
has been a wonderful experience. Today I am not so excited for
the youngster deciding to make football his career. At the start
of this book I said that there were so many things about our great
game that I didn't understand. The biggest mystery of all is why
people are scared to change when that is what we so desperately
need.

Football in this country must not just survive. We must be
brave and ambitious and plan for the future during the next
decade. We must go into the 80s with new blood and fresh
enthusiasm.

Ten years goes very quickly. Believe me.

21

You need friends

I can still see the headline now. It came out of the *News of the World* newspaper and hit me like a hard slap in the face. 'SuperFlop' it screamed in huge type over a picture of me walking dejectedly away from Wembley.

It was the morning after Arsenal's FA Cup Final defeat by Ipswich in 1978 and the headline told the world what that newspaper thought of Malcolm Macdonald's performance. As I have said before, there were no complaints from me; I have voiced my opinion all my life and would never dream of taking the right to comment away from anyone.

The headline didn't embarrass me either, and I can honestly say that I have never been upset by criticism. What it did teach me was the value of good friends. I knew why I had not done well but realized that a majority of people were dismissing me as a failure.

It wasn't worth publicly trying to explain and so I went to the people that matter to me. Losing at the very highest level in sport is a traumatic and emotional experience that few people appreciate and it is important to talk the disappointment out of your system. That, I suppose, can be related to everything in life. A husband who doesn't discuss problems with his wife has got a dead marriage on his hands.

Apart from my wife and family there is one person I continually turn to for advice and help and that is Harry Haslam. He has been with me right from the start and my mother was proved right when, after the first time she met Harry, she told me: 'That man will be like a second father to you'. It was a great character reference and Harry is someone who has always stood by me. The definition of a friend is surely someone who understands you best of all and, in football, that is HH.

He has advised, helped and criticized me along the road, and made sure others do the same. On the morning I left Luton to join Newcastle Harry telephoned Joe Harvey and I heard him say: 'Now, Joe, you look after this lad, he is a good 'un'. Harry has become one of the family.

In January 1980 the Sportsman Club in London held a tribute retirement dinner for National Hunt jockey Graham Thorner and myself and Harry paid me the compliment of motoring down from Sheffield, making a speech and travelling home again in the early hours to be ready for training. That is the kind of man Haslam is and behind his public image of joking Harry Haslam lies a very sincere person and an under-rated manager.

I was lucky to have Harry on my side at the start at Tonbridge and, even now, I am always recalling words of advice and tips he gave me all those years ago.

When I began as a right back in the Southern League I had terrible trouble with my concentration, wanting to drift up for some glory by scoring goals. Harry would say to me in the dressing room afterwards: 'What the hell are you doing, lad? You're supposed to be marking, not playing as a dual centre forward.'

One day before an important game Harry gave me two cotton-wool balls and said: 'Hold these tightly in your hands and it will help you concentrate and remember your job'. I clutched those wool balls for about four matches until I got it right and, when things were not going well in the First Division, out they came again. The Newcastle and Arsenal boys would look at me in amazement as I went down the tunnel squeezing the wool into shape.

Today I use Harry's remedy to help me plan a busy day in the office. If I have got a lot on my mind, I hold a small piece of wool in my hand as I'm driving down the M1. It helps me concentrate and forces me to remember important things. It sounds silly and corny written down but, like the knot in the handkerchief, it works.

Joe Harvey kept the promise he made to Haslam and looked after me. He was more than a manager. There was a little bit of Harry in him and he treated the Newcastle players like his sons.

Harvey is the kind of man who would get on board a boat without knowing where it was destined but then battle 24 hours a day to keep it on course. He worked those kind of hours to steer Newcastle into great times and if players stepped out of line he

didn't throw them overboard but only handed them a lifeline
and encouraged them to do even better.

I once overheard Joe talking to the waiting press boys after
Newcastle had been beaten away from home 2-1. Joe was saying:
'Yes, we lost, but didn't we play some great stuff? Terry was
magnificent, Tommy did great, it was a marvellous match.'

And that was Joe, always wanting to entertain. Unlike some
other managers who are scared of failure, Harvey didn't mind
the odd defeat as long as it was a good match. He enjoyed
watching an exciting game as much as the spectators even if we
lost. If the players and the Geordie public were happy, so was
Joe.

Two of my other close friends at Newcastle were team-mates
Frank Clark and John Tudor. Frank Clark almost did me a great
favour that could have changed the entire make-up of my life.

Frank had gone on a free transfer to Nottingham Forest and,
when he heard I was unsettled at Newcastle, called me to ask: 'If
you're moving, come to Forest. I know Cloughie is looking for a
striker and I'll put in a good word for you.'

At the time Forest were in the Second Division and I politely
turned down Frank Clark's offer because I thought I could do
better than Forest. I thought there were bigger things ahead for
me. How wrong could I be? While I will never forget the experience of playing at Arsenal, I often dream of the standards that
Forest have set since my telephone conversation with Frank.
There was no guarantee, of course, that Brian Clough would
have signed me but it is interesting to measure the small dividing
line between gaining complete success in football.

John Tudor helped me continuously on and off the field and
we spent hours chatting how we could work better as a pair. We
had practised a long time on one particular move when, in an
FA Cup tie at West Brom, it worked like a dream and John
scored with a superb header. It was tremendously satisfying to
see the move work and, with the ball safely in the net, I shouted
at Tudor: 'Now I know what you mean'. That should act as a
lesson to all youngsters in any walk of life. Always listen and take
advice from experienced people and work hard at whatever you
choose to do.

One man I have often mentioned in this book and whom I
class as a good friend is Alec Stock. I think I get on so well with
Alec because of all the people I have met he is most like me.

There is only one person who knows Alec best and that is

himself. Like me, he is a bit of a mystery. He has a very private side to his make-up that he doesn't expose. He is his own man, hates two-faced people and like Haslam and Harvey, is very loyal to his players.

Everyone who has played for Alec respects the 'old commander' although not many begin to understand him. Numerous times I have watched Alec at work in the dressing room before a game. A player often dismisses what Alec has told him but then produces his finest performance of the season. He didn't realize that Alec had just done a superb motivating job.

I'm sure a little bit of Haslam, Harvey and Stock have rubbed off on me and I'm taking those qualities into a new era of my life. I have always been my own man, although I have been prepared to listen and learn.

Even when faced with an angry supporter or a foul-mouthed yob I try and analyse what makes him behave like that. It is too easy just to scream back. Life is too short to burn energy on senseless arguing. That is why friends are vital to talk to and turn towards.

The first piece of advice I was given as a centre forward was 'Be greedy' and now my motto for anyone is 'Never be afraid to miss'. I never was afraid to miss when scoring goals. That is my approach to the rest of my life.

I am prepared to gamble in business and have a go at something I believe will make me a success and a better person. And, who knows, I might just hit the target a few more times yet.